Merton's Palace of Nowhere

"This one door is the door of the Palace of Nowhere. It is the door of God. It is our very self, our true self called by God to perfect union with himself. And it is through this door we secretly enter in responding to the saving call to 'Come with me to the Palace of Nowhere where all the many things are one.'"

— *Chapter 5, p. 151*

Merton's Palace of Nowhere

A Search for God through Awareness of the True Self

James Finley

with a Foreword by HENRI NOUWEN

AVE MARIA PRESS
NOTRE DAME, IND. 46556

Contents

Acknowledgments

My sincere thanks goes to the following people whose support and guidance made this book possible:

My close friend Father Flavian Burns, OCSO, greatly influenced the underlying tone and direction of this work. He generously shared with me his own astute insight into Thomas Merton's spirituality. Brother Patrick Hart, OCSO, was supportive of my efforts from start to finish. His editorial suggestions were most helpful.

Father Henri Nouwen was generous with both his time and enthusiastic support. John Mogabgab of Yale Divinity School made numerous editorial suggestions which were incorporated into the final text. James Andrews played a significant role in my initial decision to undertake this project. Father John Eudes Bamberger, OCSO, was helpful to me in the initial stages of the preparation of the manuscript. I am also indebted to Dom Timothy Kelly, OCSO, Abbot of Gethsemani, for his cooperation in allowing me to continue visiting the Abbey. Thanks also to Martha Oakes for help in preparation of first drafts of the manuscripts.

The following friends and colleagues read and critiqued my work: Michael Pennock, Father Don Cozzens, Sister Cathy Hilkert, Father Felix Donahue, OCSO, Father Charles McCabe, Father Edward Prendergast, John Hules and Bill Plato.

I am indebted to all who have listened to my lectures on Thomas Merton's spirituality and responded with questions and constructive criticism that occasioned the further clarification of my thoughts.

James Finley

Foreword

The only time I met Thomas Merton, I was struck by his utter earthiness. While on a retreat at the Abbey of Gethsemani, two students from the University of Notre Dame who had made an appointment to meet Merton at the lakeside asked me to join them. It was a very chatty encounter. We talked a little about abbots, a little about Camus and a little about writing. We drank beer, stared into the water and let some time pass in silence—nothing very special, profound, or "spiritual." In fact, it was a little disappointing. Maybe I had expected something unusual, something to talk about with others or to write home about. But Thomas Merton proved to be a very down-to-earth, healthy human being who was not going to perform to satisfy our curiosity. He was one of us.

Later, when I studied Merton's books, taught a course about his life and works, and wrote a short introduction to his thought, I became very grateful for that one unspectacular encounter. I found that whenever I was tempted to let myself be carried away by lofty ideas or cloudy aspirations, I had only to remind myself of that one afternoon to bring myself back to earth. When my mind's eye saw him again as that earthy man, dressed in sloppy blue jeans, loud, laughing, friendly and unpretentious, I would realize

7

that Merton was and is no more than a window through whom we may perhaps catch a glimpse of the One who had called him to a life of prayer and solitude. Every attempt to put Merton on a pedestal would not only horrify Merton himself, but would also be in direct contrast to everything for which he stood. Merton expressed this unambiguously when, after 20 years of monastic life, he wrote: "My monastery . . . . is a place in which I disappear from the world as an object of interest in order to be everywhere in it by hiddenness and compassion" (Preface to the Japanese edition of *The Seven Storey Mountain,* p. 11). To make Merton again an object of interest would be like robbing him posthumously of his vocation. It belonged to the essence of his vocation to let the old "interested and interesting" self die and to receive a new self which is hidden in God.

Why, then, another book on Merton? Not because Merton was so interesting and unusual, but because he was and still is an excellent guide in our search for God. James Finley, who lived with Merton for six years, has "used" Merton in the only way Merton was willing to be used: as a guide on our way to God. This book is, therefore, not primarily about Merton. Rather, it is a book about our spiritual journey, for which Merton offers ideas, suggestions and necessary encouragement, but in which he never becomes the object of interest himself.

Merton is a good guide. He felt our times well, and he was a perceptive observer of the many ups and downs in the spiritual struggles of contemporary men and women. With his remarkable literary talent, Merton was able to articulate his outer and inner worlds in such a way that his fellow travelers discovered in him an excellent interpreter of their own experiences and a good friend to help them find the way through often unknown territory.

In this book, a choice has been made. James Finley

has chosen to lift out of Merton's works the theme of our quest for a spiritual identity, a theme which can be found in the spiritual writings of all Christian centuries, but which has received a new emphasis in our days. James Finley describes the spiritual life as the long and often arduous journey on which we slowly become detached from our false, illusory self—a self that is little more than the collective evaluations and affirmations of our surroundings—and are opened up to receive a new self that is participation in the life of God. In this journey that we all must make if we take our search for God seriously, Merton proves to be an excellent guide not only because he knows the Christian tradition so well, but also because his study of Eastern Mysticism had given him words to articulate in a fresh, often playful and humorous, way this eternal quest for our true identity. James Finley has made full use of Merton's rich knowledge of the West and the East and so has been able to give his study the same broad perspective which is so characteristic of Merton's later work.

I hope that all those who read this very insightful book will be able to detach themselves more and more from the desire to know Merton and become more and more open to receive the knowledge of God's presence in their lives. I am sure that this would please not only Thomas Merton, but James Finley as well.

Henri J. M. Nouwen

Introduction: Upon Learning to See

I

This book is a series of prayerful explorations into the spirituality of Thomas Merton. More specifically, it is an attempt to pass on a gift that I received during some six years as a monk at the Trappist monastery of Our Lady of Gethsemani. The daily monastic life and my personal contact with Father Louis (Merton's monastic name) as my novice master were priceless graces which I feel moved to share with those who feel drawn to some degree of contemplative union with God.

It is they who seek union with God in prayer who have found a light and guide in the person of Thomas Merton. He said of himself that he had but one desire and that was ". . . the desire for solitude—to disappear into God . . . to be lost in the secret of His Face."[1] Merton's whole life was the living out of that desire, actualized through daily fidelity to solitude, silence and prayer. He wrote out of the substance of his life and became known to the world through his charism for articulating something of the ineffable reality of the living God. Over the years many readers have drawn strength from his words by recognizing in Merton their own craving for God. He says what they themselves have experienced but do not know how to express. In short, to his many readers, Merton reveals himself as an elder brother on the lonely path to God, a mystic, one in whom the otherness of God becomes Emmanuel.

We turn to Merton in the hope that he can aid us in our life of prayer. Such a hope can be fulfilled only if we accept beforehand the subtle, delicate nature of prayer itself. Prayer emerges from, and leads to, a certain *way* of knowing which is most difficult to communicate in words. The immediacy of the experience makes communication of it all but impossible. It is much like trying to describe the taste of salt to someone who has never tasted it.

With prayer this difficulty is heightened even more, for the encounter with God in prayer is, like love and death, always an unexpected and unprecedented event. Here we must respect the ineffable quality of the reality which we seek to explore. In other words, we must not look for the wrong *kind* of certitude as we approach Merton as a guide in the ways of prayer. As he himself tells us,

> . . . contemplation does not simply "find" a clear idea of God and confine Him within the limits of that idea, and hold Him there as a prisoner to whom it can always return. On the contrary, contemplation is carried away by Him into His own realm, His own mystery and His own freedom. It is a pure and virginal knowledge, poor in concepts, poorer still in reasoning, but able, by its very poverty and purity, to follow the Word "wherever He may go."[2]

It would no doubt be pushing the reader's tolerance too far to suggest that we are here going to work in never-ending circles of paradox upon paradox. But, hopefully, the reader will have little trouble accepting the simple fact that the ways of prayer often call forth a kind of knowing that passes beyond clear ideas and the ordinary way of thinking.

Any serious, daily practice of interior prayer will give some taste of the following experience: You sit in prayer. On the surface there is nothing. Yet, as the noise of your next thought falls away, as you allow the silence to deepen around and within you, you discover that you are on the trackless waters on which Jesus bid Peter to walk in order to be united with him. To use the imagery of Saint John of the Cross, there is a path to walk with "no light except the one that burns in your heart." You set out to find him who calls you out of nothingness to union with himself. You set out knowing that you must find God, yet the first step leaves you lost. An inner wisdom tells you that "to reach him whom you do not know you must go by a way you do not know."

Prayer as described here never touches us as long as it remains on the surface of our lives, as long as it is nothing but one more of the thousand things that must be done. It is only when prayer becomes "the one thing necessary" that real prayer begins. Prayer begins to take on its full dimensions only when we begin to intuit that the subtle nothingness of prayer is everything. Prayer begins when we go to our place of prayer as to a sacred place, when we realize that our own heart is the place where Jacob's ladder touches the earth.

In prayer we sit and we are lost before we begin. Prayer appears before us as a kind of palace with no doors. The palace is nowhere and the path leading to it has no sign saying "enter here." We find ourselves in a solitary silence that skirts the edge of the abyss that is at once our own nothingness and the plenitude of God. In prayer, if we follow it through far enough, we eventually come face to face with the fundamental question of life—How can we find him who fills all things yet evades our grasp? How can we find our way to the Father?

Of course, for the Christian, Jesus is the Way to the Father. We know this; we celebrate this in liturgy; we give thanks for the gift of faith in which we are empowered to say "Jesus is Lord" and to experience his presence in our lives. But Christianity is more than thanking God for going out of himself to unite himself to us in Christ. We must also go out to meet Christ. And going out to meet Christ is more than simply serving others and faithfully fulfilling external observances.

We are called upon to live Christ's life. We are called into the desert to meet the demon within. We are called to face God alone in the night of our own solitude. We are called to die with Jesus, in order to live with him. We are asked to lose all, to be emptied out, in order to be filled with the very fullness of God.

Therefore, the Christian surely knows the way to the Father, but for this knowledge to become true, life-giving knowledge, each Christian must find his or her own way to the Way which is Christ. Christianity is much more than an expression of brotherly love couched in religious terms. It is more than philanthropy with holy water on it. It is essential that each person make some kind of personal response to God in Christ. There is a risk to take. There is a journey to make.

Here on earth, few are called to a full contemplative awareness of the reality that awaits each of us after death. But all who desire union with Christ are bound to seek the degree of prayer that is willed by God for them to achieve. For some people their response to Christ may involve only a minimal degree of interior realization of their union with God and others in Christ. For others, however, they know they simply must pray and pray with all their hearts if they are ever to become the person God wills them to be. It is to just such people that Merton spoke in his clearest voice.

But in turning to pray such people confront the per-plexity referred to above. In solitary prayer we find our-selves facing the dilemma of having to do what we are incapable of doing. It is like the situation created by the Zen master who tells the aspirant to "just sit." The aspirant quickly discovers that he or she can sit and do many things: sit and sleep, sit and think, sit and wonder, sit and wonder why one cannot stop wondering. But to *just* sit is beyond us. Our own ingrained complexity makes the simplest of acts the most difficult to achieve.

It is out of this kind of practical, pressing necessity that many have turned for direction to Merton's writings on prayer. And it goes without saying that many have found what they were looking for. Merton fulfills his own criterion for a director as one who offers "kindly support and wise advice," one who "enables us to *accept* more per-fectly what we already know and see in an obscure way," or sometimes helps us to see "things which we have hitherto been unable to see, though they were staring us in the face."[3]

But at the fundamental level of prayer itself Merton has no solutions to the problems of prayer. He tells us frankly that with prayer itself "the only One who can teach me to find God is God Himself, Alone."[4]

Merton never offers us any surefire techniques as a solution to prayer. There is no Merton method to prayer. He makes clear that the whole matter of finding God lies not in asking God questions but in being humble enough and open enough to abandon ourselves to the life-and-death question which God asks of us. He writes of his own experience of God:

> God, My God, God whom I meet in dark-ness, with You it is always the same thing! Always

the same question that nobody knows how to answer!

I have prayed to You in the daytime with thoughts and reasons, and in the nighttime You have confronted me scattering thought and reason. I have come to You in the morning with light and with desire, and You have descended upon me, with great gentleness, with most forbearing silence, in this inexplicable night, dispersing light, defeating all desire. I have explained to You a hundred times my motives for entering the monastery and You have listened and said nothing, and I have turned away and wept with shame.[5]

There could be no greater disservice than that of sparing someone from this necessary and often painful dimension of prayer. Merton writes,

Let no one hope to find in contemplation an escape from conflict, from anguish, or from doubt. On the contrary, the deep inexpressible certitude of the contemplative experience awakens a tragic anguish and opens many questions in the depth of the heart like wounds that cannot stop bleeding.[6]

Merton would not deliver us from this purifying darkness, for in it is born the light we seek. In it we discover that the question we ask "is itself the answer. And we ourselves are both (the question and the answer)."[7] In this darkness we bleed as one with Christ, who emptying himself upon the cross turned emptiness into fullness and death into life.

The way to our deliverance is what we fear the most. There is something in us that constantly tries to latch on to an answer and close in upon it like a hungry starfish encircling a clam to suck from it all the "spiritual riches" that we hunger for.

Merton would tell us that techniques and spiritualities are proper and necessary in their own right, but we must not ask from them what we can only receive from God. Chanting OM with great enthusiasm for hours on end may well be an efficacious exercise in meditation. However, it may also be but a sign of a weird person. Or, worse yet, it may be a way of tricking ourselves into believing that some contrivance of our own making can of itself take us to God.

Merton would assure us that progress in prayer is always a gift. God is always beyond our cleverest plans. He is not to be flushed into the open by beating the bushes with well-wrought aphorisms. But in a simple abandonment to his will we find that, like our next breath, he is upon us, that he engulfs us and holds us fast.

Merton moves as the wind moves. Like a spiritual gadfly, like a thief in the night, his *Raids on the Unspeakable* leaves us few clues, save our own reawakened awareness of God. He leaves impoverished the schemer and the organizer within us. But the child in us, the self in us that prays, finds itself fed with *Bread in the Wilderness*.[8]

There is no attempt here to alleviate the paradoxical language and evasive quality of Merton's words. This is why the opening lines of this introduction intentionally identify our task here as that of making prayerful explorations into Merton's thought. We do not come to analyze Merton's teaching, but rather to savor his words in that same intuitive receptivity in which his writings rose to consciousness from the depths of his own soul. Here we are not going to dissect Merton's thought, but rather, as it were, prayerfully roll his words over and over in our hands, trying to grasp now this, now that facet of light thrown into the darkness that surrounds the meeting place with God. We can only hope to create that empty space, that context for insight in which the unexpected everything can rise mysteriously and effortlessly out of the nothingness in which we wait for God. Reading in this way brings us to the heart of what is traditionally known as spiritual reading.

Spiritual reading has the potential of becoming itself a prayer, a kind of event in which a true transformation of consciousness takes place. At times like these the reading takes on a sacramental force that transforms the silence of a room, the wind, a flower, the ticking of a clock into sudden, subtle and unexpected manifestations of God, silently calling from the midst of things to "be still and know that I am God."

In the reader's simple, humble desire for God the words are empowered to unveil a fleeting glimpse of life's most secret meaning. One's own innermost, unspoken insights and desires are suddenly encountered on the printed page. The response is a deepening of those desires and a renewed courage to set out for still deeper waters.

II

The underlying thesis of this work is that Merton's whole spirituality, in one way or another, pivots on the question of ultimate human identity. Merton's message is that we are one with God. What Merton repeatedly draws us to is the realization that our own deepest self is not so much our own self as it is the self one with the "Risen and Deathless Christ in Whom all are fulfilled in One."[9]

Merton leads us along the journey to God in which the self that begins the journey is not the self that arrives. The self that begins is the self that we thought ourselves to be. It is this self that dies along the way until in the end "no one" is left. This "no one" is our true self. It is the self that stands prior to all that is this or that. It is the self in God, the self bigger than death yet born of death. It is the self the Father forever loves.

We can now say that a more specific purpose underlying this book is that of prayerfully exploring Merton's
critically important yet little-appreciated notion of *the true
self in God* as opposed to *the false self of egocentric desires.*
The task before us is a prayerful asking of Who Am I, not
relative to this or that aspect of my being, but rather who
am I *ultimately* before God? The question is, in other
words, who am I *absolutely?* It is obvious that based on
experience I know who I am by virtue of my relationships
with others: relative to my parents I know myself as son,
relative to my wife as husband, and so forth, with each of
the relationships, both past and present, that have gone into
the making of what I call my personality. The identity
given to me by these relationships is certainly real enough,
but none of these relationships either individually or collec-
tively constitutes the totality of my being. None of the relationships referred to above gave me my very existence, but
rather found me as already existing, and from there helped
to mold for better or for worse my empirical identity. Even
my parents, though the causes of my biological existence,
did not create the unique core of my being, but rather discovered me as a newly unfolding mystery in their midst.

Merton makes no attempt to question the reality and
importance of the empirical self we call our personality.
Indeed, in the spiritual life a deep respect must be given to
our whole person, including the day-by-day realities of life
and the self that is formed by them. What Merton does
say, however, is that when the relative identity of the ego is
taken to be my deepest and only identity, when I am
thought to be nothing but the sum total of all my relationships, when I cling to this self and make it the center around
which and for which I live, I then make my empirical identity into the false self. My own self then becomes the
obstacle to realizing my true self.

The true self is not some obscure and hidden identity

that we must pull forth from the darkness like a rabbit from a hat. Nor is it some evasive entity running lost in the labyrinths of our minds. The true self is rather our whole self before God. It is the self the Father created us to become. It is the self in Christ. It is the self that breathes, that stands and sits. It is the self that is. The true self, being simple like God, can be realized only in the mode of simple awareness proper to it. This mode of awareness is nothing other than the contemplative awareness referred to in the first part of this introduction. This is why the two elements of contemplative awareness and the search for the true self are inseparably entwined together. An exploration of the true self will bring us to an understanding of prayer and a prayerful attentiveness will bring us to an understanding of the true self. That is to say, the self that prays truly is the true self. It is in prayer that we discover our own deepest reality from which we have strayed like runaway children becoming strangers to ourselves.

The spirituality of Thomas Merton centers upon the fact that the whole of the spiritual life finds its fulfillment in bringing our entire life into a transforming, loving communion with the ineffable God. This communion is both the *raison d'etre* and fruition of our deepest self. In fact, this communion reveals that we ourselves are ineffable, being made in the image and likeness of God and called to a union of identity with God forever.

Such a communion is beyond what words can say, but a prayerful, respectful pursuit of Merton's understanding of the true self can bring us to the brink of the insight into our own ultimate identity as radically one with God in Christ. This insight, which is itself a gift, will provide us with the unifying vision that is expressed not only in Merton but in all the great mystical traditions as well.

What Merton says of the insight proper to Zen is applicable to our present task.

> . . . the way to see it is not first to define Zen and
> then apply the definition. . . The real way to
> study Zen is to penetrate the outer shell and taste
> the inner kernel which cannot be defined. Then
> one realizes in oneself the reality which is being
> talked about.[10]

In this same passage Merton continues by offering a
Zen Mondo to make his point.

> A Zen Master said to his disciple: "Go get my
> rhinoceroshorn fan."
>
> Disciple: "Sorry, Master, it is broken."
>
> Master: "Okay, then get me the rhinoceros."

If we can realize at the beginning that we are presented
with an impossible task, if we can save ourselves the illusion
that we can pick away at a few words and find the reality
simply because we have figured out what is being said, then
we can perhaps allow ourselves to become humble enough,
patient enough and silent enough that as we read of the
rhinoceros we will feel his hot breath on the back of our
necks. This is the way of discovery proper to finding the
true self. As Merton himself wisely counsels us:

> The inner self is as secret as God and, like
> him, it evades every concept that tries to seize
> hold of it with full possession. It is a life that
> cannot be held and studied as object, because it
> it not "a thing." It is not reached and coaxed
> forth from hiding by any process under the sun,
> including meditation. All that we can do with
> any spiritual discipline is produce within our-
> selves something of the silence, the humility, the
> detachment, the purity of heart and the indiffer-
> ence which are required if the inner self is to
> make some shy, unpredictable manifestation of
> his presence.[11]

One final word of caution may help alleviate some possible misunderstanding later. The quest for God is centered wholly upon God and not upon the various thoughts and feelings we may happen to have along the way. Prayer brings us into a vital, ineffable, lived-out participation in Jesus' cross and resurrection. The whole gamut of human experience is drawn into this faith encounter. Yet, the experiences are but the waves splashing up on a distant shore. They are but the ripples in the sand left by the retreating tide.

Our psychological reactions and experiences must wisely be taken into account, but at no time must such experiences blind us to what they point to and express, which is precisely that union beyond all possible experience and expression. Thus, in the pages that follow we will speak often of sorrow, but this sorrow is not to be equated with emotional despondency. Likewise, the joy that erupts within is not wild exhilaration that makes us run around on the ceiling. Joy, sorrow and all similar expressions that are referred to in the following pages refer not to emotional states but to penetrating, subtle realizations of our most fundamental relationship to God. Joy and sorrow may at times spill over into the emotions, but this is all a matter of temperament. It is all accidental to the reality of the loving God who moves mysteriously within us, transforming our hearts into the likeness of his Son.

The spiritual life is to be earnestly pursued as though no spiritual life existed. This is the only safe and sane way to travel in the deep waters of the Spirit. Indeed, such childlike simplicity in the face of God expresses a realization that there is, in fact, no spiritual life as such separate from life itself. There is only one life, and that is God's life which he gives to us from moment to moment, drawing us to himself with every holy breath we take. The purpose of our prayer is to help us find God, that we might consciously and gratefully live this life, and through our presence invite others to live it as well.

1. The Foundation of the False Self

I

The terms "true self" and "false self" are not the creations of Merton, in the sense in which the term "unconscious" is the creation of Freud or the phrase *"cogito ergo sum"* is unique to Descartes. Merton's spirituality is firmly grounded in Christian revelation and tradition. His genius lies not in founding a new spirituality, nor in coining his own unique concepts, but in drawing forth unrecognized and unappreciated, yet vitally important, elements from various traditions. He brings these elements together in new configurations more meaningful to contemporary man.

We will begin this chapter by indicating briefly the scriptural and sacramental basis for what Merton terms the false self.

In Genesis we see that the foundation of our life and identity resides in our unique, life-giving relationship with God. Likewise, in Genesis we see that the archetypal disobedience of Adam and Eve has caused our spiritual death by damaging our relationship with God.

From very early in Israel's history there is planted in her heart a seed of hope for deliverance from this self-inflicted bondage to death. Israel yearns for a Messiah.

She cries out to God for deliverance and her cry is answered in the person of Jesus.

"In the beginning," the opening line of the Gospel of John, clearly echoes the opening line of Genesis. New Testament texts make clear that, in Jesus, our origins begin anew. By Jesus' acceptance of the Father's will he has restored our relationship with God. Jesus, the New Adam, gives birth to the New Man by giving to mankind the Spirit in whom Jesus is one with the Father. Jesus takes the effects of Adam's disobedience upon himself and in his death "death dies." Jesus, in resurrected glory, appears before us as the firstfruits of a new humankind whose life is once again grounded in God, in whom there is no death.

Christian life is clearly presented in the New Testament to be primarily a participation in the life of Christ. We are called "to die with him" by "dying to sin" so that we might "rise with him." Life in Christ does not then begin at biological death, but rather begins now in a death to self, in a conversion, a *metanoia,* in which we "put on the mind of Christ" and live a life through Christ in the Spirit. Thus Paul says that "if anyone is in Christ, he is a new creation. The old order has passed away; now all is new!" (2 Cor 5:17).

This reality is made sacramentally present within the believing community by the initiation rite of Baptism. The early Christian practice of adult baptism by immersion gave graphic symbolic expression to this sharing in the death and resurrection of Christ. The writings of the Fathers speak of the waters of Baptism as both a womb and a tomb. The one being baptized goes down into the water as Christ went down into the earth in death. The coming up out of the water is Christ rising in glory, victorious over death. In Baptism the Spirit, given entrance through faith, incorporates the Christian into Christ's life. Christ's life becomes our own so that we can say with Paul, "for me to live is Christ."

But our daily life and our prayer quickly reveal to us that our life in Christ is a life in becoming. Christ is the door that leads to life, but we ourselves must walk through that door by sharing in his death in order to share in his life. This calls for a daily and sometimes arduous struggle, a daily carrying of our cross which is, above all, our own deeply seated rebellion against God and our resulting tendency toward death. This tendency to sin and death is itself a mystery. It is the darkness that has been redeemed by Christ but which we must constantly and with effort bring to his healing gaze. It is sin. It is what Merton calls the false self.

II

We pursue the spiritual life as children of Adam struggling to give birth to the new and original self given to us by God and restored to us by Christ. We struggle as though in labor. From the rich soil of our hopes there spring forth only thorns. The tiniest flower demands our sweat before it appears through the rocky ground. We spend our nights in weeping and our days in toil. We strive to grow beyond ourselves, to give birth to Christ's life within us.

We are like the hideous man Merton presents to us in *The Way of Chuang Tzu:*

> When a hideous man becomes a father
> And a son is born to him
> In the middle of the night
> He trembles and lights a lamp
> And runs to look in anguish
> On that child's face
> To see whom he resembles.[1]

Each day we rise from prayer and rush to the mirror of self-awareness in the hope of discovering that our efforts have given birth to the image of someone who does not bear the mark of our disfigurement. Each day we hope to discover the face of a child born anew. But left to our own devices we discover only the old man of misguided self-seeking. Adam lives within us. In his disobedience unto death we behold ourselves. Our daily actions, our blindness in prayer, reveal to us that the wound dealt upon the human heart still pulses and festers within us.

The core of our being is drawn like a stone to the quiet depths of each moment where God waits for us with eternal longing. But to those depths the false self will not let us travel. Like stones skipped across the surface of the water we are kept skimming along the peripheral, one-dimensional fringes of life. To sink is to vanish. To sink into the unknown depths of God's call to union with himself is to lose all that the false self knows and cherishes.

Thus, the false self does not face or even acknowledge the darkness within. On the contrary, the darkness is proclaimed to be the brightest of lights. The false self, like a ruling despot, demands unquestioning obedience. Everything must be kept moving in an endless cult of domination and exploitation.

But, while turning from the ways of the false self to the path of interior prayer, we find ourselves on the horns of a dilemma which is finally resolved only in a childlike abandonment to God's mercy. On the one hand there is the great truth that from the first moment of my existence the deepest dimension of my life is that I am made by God for union with himself. The deepest dimension of my identity as a human person is that I share in God's own life both now and in eternity in a relationship of untold intimacy.

On the other hand, my own daily experience impresses

upon me the painful truth that my heart has listened to the serpent instead of to God. There is something in me that puts on fig leaves of concealment, kills my brother, builds towers of confusion, and brings cosmic chaos upon the earth. There is something in me that loves darkness rather than light, that rejects God and thereby rejects my own deepest reality as a human person made in the image and likeness of God.

Sin is the word we most often use to refer to this latter aspect of human experience in which we find ourselves negating our own intrinsic relationship to God. Sin taken in this sense does not, of course, refer simply to the isolated actions which we call sinful. Rather, such actions are seen as symptoms or manifestations of sin taken as the state or condition of alienation in which we find ourselves. As Paul expresses it in Romans, ". . . I am weak flesh sold unto slavery of sin. I cannot understand my own actions. I do not do what I want to do but what I hate. . . . What happens is that I do, not the good I will to do, but the evil I do not intend. But if I do what is against my will, it is not I who do it, but sin which dwells in me" (Rom 7:14-20).

Of sin considered in this way, Merton writes:

> To say I was born in sin is to say I came into the world with a false self. I was born in a mask. I came into existence under a sign of contradiction, being someone that I was never intended to be and therefore a denial of what I am supposed to be. And thus I came into existence and nonexistence at the same time because from the very start I was something that I was not.[2]

Here Merton equates sin with the identity-giving structures of the false self. This in itself is significant. The focus of sin is shifted from the realm of morality to that of ontology. For Merton, the matter of *who* we are always precedes what we do. Thus, sin is not essentially an action but rather an identity. Sin is a fundamental stance of wanting to be what we are not. Sin is thus an orientation to falsity, a basic lie concerning our own deepest reality. Likewise, inversely, to turn away from sin is, above all, to turn away from a tragic case of mistaken identity concerning our own selves.

This then is the false self. It is a tragic self, in that it ends up with less than nothing in trying to gain more than the everything which God freely bestows upon his children. The false self is a whole syndrome of lies and illusions that spring from a radical rejection of God in whom alone we find our own truth and ultimate identity.

With this background in mind we can now reflect upon Merton's insights into Adam as the paradigm of the false self. We will more readily be able to understand what is meant by the term the "true self" if we can put our finger on precisely what is false in the false self. But, before proceeding with these and later reflections on Adam in Merton's writings, we would do well to keep in mind that Merton approaches Adam not as a biblical scholar but rather as a spokesman of the Christian contemplative traditions. The Genesis text itself tells us that we are sharers in divine life as God's creatures, that we were created to find our fulfillment in our faithful response to God.

The biblical meaning of this text is left intact yet developed by the reflections of later Christian writers of the various patristic, monastic and contemplative traditions. In the light of Christ (the New Adam) and from within the context of contemplative experience (in the Spirit) the Adam and Eve narrative provides a rich source of symbols revealing to us our call from God in creation to become perfectly like him through Christ in the Spirit. It is in continuity with these Christian traditions that Merton turns to Adam in his reflections on the true self in God.

III

Prayer, understood as the distilled awareness of our entire life before God, is a journey forward, a response to a call from the Father to become perfectly like his Son through the power of the Holy Spirit. But this journey forward can also be seen as a kind of journey backward, in which we seek to gain access to the relationship Adam had with God.

In prayer we journey forward to our origin. We close our eyes in prayer and open them in the pristine moment of creation. We open our eyes to find God, his hands still smeared with clay, hovering over us, breathing into us his own divine life, smiling to see in us a reflection of himself. We go to our place of prayer confident that in prayer we transcend both place and time.

In prayer, distinctions like outside and inside, past and future, no longer apply. In prayer, we sit before the gates of Eden and the self the Father created us to be appears, freed from layer upon layer of falsity and distortion in which we had become entangled and lost. In prayer, we experience this going back to our origins as a going into the center of our self, where God holds both our origin and end in one eternal moment.

Our journey back is thus not a chronological one, going back as a psychiatrist might take his patient to a past event that caused some particular disorientation at the psychological level. It is worth noting, however, that our psychological wholeness is in no way removed from our growth in prayer. The true self is the whole self. A life of prayer involves an integrated wholeness of our entire life before God. We must learn to discover the wounded father and mother living within. We must learn to heal them and at the same time "hate them" by not drawing our life and identity from them, but rather from the Father who ever draws us forward into a land "we know not," yet a land which is our only true home.

Adam is not seen as some historical figure who committed a particular act that brought about a kind of ontological birth defect that is handed down from child to child. Rather, Adam is now. Adam is ourselves in disobedience to God. The garden of Eden prior to the fall is just as much in the future as it is in the past. As we said, the depths of the heart know no time. Both heaven and hell live not only beyond us but also within us, and it is through the door of ourselves that we enter into both.

Considering Adam as an archetypal mirror of ourselves, we see God calling us out of nothingness, drawing us forth from the chaos to give us a relationship of likeness to himself. He breathes into us his own divine life and makes it our own. But God does not sweep over us like a tidal wave. Rather, with power and yet with a divine meekness, he invites us to respond to his call by giving ourselves to him with that same abandonment with which he gives himself to us. It is our love for God that makes us most like God. He asks for our love, our self-donation, in the intimate life-giving encounter with himself that will later be more definitively expressed in terms of *faith* and *covenant*.

Genesis also tells of a serpent who lies about a promise of divinity to God's children. The serpent's promise is a venom that flows into the vibrant, delicate faith bond between ourselves and God. The serpent, midwife of the false self, injects its poisonous promises into Adam's desire to be like God. This fact alone reveals something of the paradox and mystery of evil, for the serpent's lie is a dark and twisted echo of God's creative act in which he made us sharers of his own divine life. Indeed, for us to want to be like God is simply for us to want to be who God created us to be in his own image and likeness. In short, Adam's desire to be like God springs from the very core of his God-given, God-created identity.

The crux of the matter is, however, that *we cannot be like God without God.* We cannot be like God by usurping God's transcendent sovereignty in a spiritual *coup* that violates God's will. We cannot take our deepest self, which is a gift from God, and wrench it from God's hands to claim it as a coveted possession.

Any expression of self-proclaimed likeness to God is forbidden us, not because it breaks some law arbitrarily decreed by God, but because such an action is tantamount to a fundamental, death-dealing, ontological lie. We are not God. We are not our own origin, nor are we our own ultimate fulfillment. To claim to be so is a suicidal act that wounds our faith relationship with the living God and replaces it with a futile faith in a self that can never exist.

And yet it is this suicidal act that the brazen liar invites Adam to commit—and Adam accepts the offer! In doing so, Adam, in effect, decapitates himself. He tears out his own heart. He gives birth to that sinister child of darkness and death that we are here referring to as the false self, the identity that Merton describes as "someone that I was never intended to be and therefore a denial of what I am supposed to be."

The spiritual life for Merton moves within the context of an identity given to us by God, distorted and hidden by sin and returned to us by Christ. The spiritual life for Merton is a journey in which we discover ourselves in discovering God, and discover God in discovering our true self hidden in God. Merton repeatedly reminds us that we must discover for ourselves what the fallen Adam within us can never see, namely, that,

> The secret of my identity is hidden in the love and mercy of God.

> But whatever is in God is really identical
> with Him, for his infinite simplicity admits no
> division and no distinction. Therefore, I cannot
> hope to find myself anywhere except in Him.

> Ultimately the only way that I can be myself
> is to become identified with Him in whom is hid-
> den the reason and fulfillment of my existence.

> Therefore, there is only one problem on
> which all my existence, my peace and my hap-
> piness depend: to discover myself in discovering
> God. If I find Him I will find myself and if I find
> my true self I will find Him.[3]

Our one problem resides in our turning, like Adam,
away from the relationship established in the total self-
donation of faith. We choose freely to reject God's way of
becoming who God calls us to become, and in this rejection
we lose our way. We lose both God and ourselves. We
choose a life outside God's love and thus choose death. We
choose a freedom outside God's will and thus lose all freedom in the narrow confines of a self that can never exist.
So it is that the spiritual life centers around the one problem of an identity found in faith. Our true self is a self in
communion. It is a self that subsists in God's eternal love.
Likewise, the false self is the self that stands outside this
created subsisting communion with God that forms our
very identity. As Merton puts it,

> When we seem to possess and use our being
> and natural faculties in a completely autonomous
> manner, as if our individual ego were the pure
> source and end of our own acts, then we are in
> illusion and our acts, however spontaneous they
> may seem to be, lack spiritual meaning and
> authenticity.[4]

In our zeal to become the landlords of our own being, we cling to each achievement as a kind of verification of our self-proclaimed reality. We become the center and God somehow recedes to an invisible fringe. Others become real to the extent they become significant others to the designs of our own ego. And in this process the ALL of God dies in us and the sterile nothingness of our desires becomes our God.

In the following text Merton makes clear that the self-proclaimed autonomy of the false self is but an illusion. He also identifies this illusion with sin and with the blindness of the world understood in Christian terms as the place that was unable to recognize Christ. This illusion, this shadow, this sin, this world, Merton states to be within us all.

Every one of us is shadowed by an illusory person: a false self.

This is the man I want myself to be but who cannot exist, because God does not know anything about him. And to be unknown of God is altogether too much privacy.

My false and private self is the one who wants to exist outside the reach of God's will and God's love—outside of reality and outside of life. And such a self cannot help but be an illusion.

We are not very good at recognizing illusions, least of all the ones we cherish about ourselves—the ones we are born with and which feed the roots of sin. For most people in the world, there is no greater subjective reality than this false self of theirs, which cannot exist. A life devoted to the cult of this shadow is what is called a life of sin.[5]

The primordial event of Adam's fall continues to live in every act we make in service of the false self. In contrast to this, the spiritual life of the Christian is a life in Christ, through whom we are enabled to remove the shackles of sin and the mask of illusion. In Christ we find the hope of a face-to-face relationship with God, in which is hidden the self he created us to become. The discovery of the true self in God takes place in the daily unfolding of Christian life. It is obscurely revealed to us in faith through selfless service to others and in the inner desert of wordless prayer.

IV

Merton sometimes speaks of Adam's fall in terms of Adam falling through the center of himself, thus placing himself between himself and God. Following upon this image we can say that not only does the false self stand between the true self and God but that the false self quickly begins to construct its own dark universe of disorientated nothingness which it claims as its prized creation and crowning glory. Merton writes,

> After Adam had passed through the center of himself and emerged on the other side to escape from God by putting himself between himself and God, he had mentally reconstructed the whole universe in his own image and likeness. That is the painful and useless labor which has been inherited by his descendants—the labor of science without wisdom; the mental toil that pieces together fragments that never manage to coalesce in one completely integrated whole: the labor of action without contemplation, that never ends in peace or satisfaction, since no task is finished without opening the way to ten more tasks that have to be done.[6]

We run and run in our squirrel cage, thinking the constant squeaking of the wheel of our achievements is a verification of our reality and worth. But in actual fact our frantic efforts to move on to the 10 more tasks that have to be done are nothing but a last-ditch effort to drown out the haunting fears that surreptitiously twist like a will-o'-the-wisp about all our happy hours.

The false self, sensing its fundamental unreality, begins to clothe itself in myths and symbols of power. Since it intuits that it is but a shadow, that it *is* nothing, it begins to convince itself that it *is* what it *does*. Hence, the more it does, achieves and experiences, the more real it becomes. Merton writes,

> All sin starts from the assumption that my false self, the self that exists only in my own egocentric desires, is the fundamental reality of life to which everything else in the universe is ordered. Thus I use up my life in the desire for pleasures and the thirst for experiences, for power, honor, knowledge, and love to clothe this false self and construct its nothingness into something objectively real. And I wind experiences around myself and cover myself with pleasures and glory like bandages in order to make myself perceptible to myself and to the world, as if I were an invisible body that could only become visible when something visible covered its surface.[7]

But the success of this adventure is always a temporary one. We lie alone like a child in the dark who is afraid there is a monster under his bed. The child is afraid to look under his bed because he knows full well that should he do so and actually find a monster he would be faced with an irreversible and unthinkable crisis. And so he prefers to whistle a tune rather than look. So, too, the false self knows that if it would become silent within and without, it would discover itself to be nothing. It would be left with nothing but its own nothingness, and to the false self which claims to be everything, such a discovery would be its undoing.

Thus, most of us cannot bear very much misanthropic self-reflection. Much of the time, the disguise is kept carefully guarded. But in the end death unveils in us what we could not bear even to acknowledge—our own radical contingency. Eventually and inevitably that which was too awful even to think about finally happens. Death reveals in us that eventually tomorrow is today and that we have run out of time. We discover by force of death that

> There is no substance under the things with which I am clothed. I am hollow, and my structure of pleasure and ambitions has no foundation. I am objectified in them. But they are all destined by their very contingency to be destroyed. And when they are gone there will be nothing left of me but my own nakedness and emptiness and hollowness, to tell me that I am my own mistake.[8]

The following text about Adam directly links the "menace of death" with the primary threat to the false self:

> Since he decided to depend on himself without contact with God, Adam had to become his own poor fallible little god. Everything now had to serve him, since he no longer served the Creator. But precisely, since he no longer fitted perfectly into the order in which they had all been established together, all creatures rebelled against Adam, and he found himself surrounded not with supports but with so many reasons for anxiety, insecurity, and fear. He was no longer able to control even his own body, which became to

some extent the master of his soul. His mind,
now, since it no longer served God, toiled in the
service of the body, wearing itself out in the
schemes to clothe and feed and gratify the flesh
and protect its frail existence against the constant menace of death.[9]

By placing the birth of the false self in the context of
Adam's journey through the center of himself, it stands to
reason that passing back through the center of ourselves is
our way of regaining our own true identity. And this is
exactly what Merton tells us; namely, that the whole of the
spiritual life can be seen as an undoing of Adam's destruc-
tive journey which brought about the dualistic, schizoid
existence of the false self as it stands over against itself, at
odds with itself and God:

If we would return to God, and find ourselves in Him, we must reverse Adam's journey,
we must go back by the way he came. The path
lies through the center of our own soul. Adam
withdrew into himself from God and then passed
through himself and went forth into creation. We
must withdraw ourselves (in the right and Christian sense) from exterior things, and pass through
the center of our souls to find God. We must
recover possession of our true selves by liberation
from anxiety and fear and inordinate desire.[10]

Here Merton turns the search for our original identity
into the basic dynamic of the spiritual life: If in my deepest
self I am a relationship to God—by whom, in whom and
for whom I exist—and if, from where I now stand, I am
in ignorance of this relationship grounded in God, then it
must follow that I stand in a radical alienation and disorientation from my own deepest identity. All ascetical strivings
can be reduced to the experience of the prodigal son who

attempts to journey back home, to return in earnest to the Father's house. By this forward journey back to one's original identity in God we reverse Adam's journey by allowing God to purify us from all that stands in opposition to his will.

A flame is not burned by itself. But we, being other than ourselves, are burned by ourselves. We eat at ourselves and consume ourselves with doubt and self-hate. We live in a shadow existence in which we find ourselves between ourselves and God. As helpless observers, we watch ourselves living out a life we know to be a fragmented tragedy. Adam's separation of himself from God dealt us a wound that each of us picks at and keeps inflamed through our daily rounds of self-deception and evasion.

In the text just cited above, Merton gives some hint of the necessity for silence and solitude in the spiritual life. By means of silence and solitude we journey into ourselves. We roam about into ever deeper, darker and more unknown realms of the human heart, wherein is found the door through which the Adam in us walked in giving birth to the false self. How can we find this door? How are we to open it? More mysterious still is the question of who will be left when the self we think ourselves to be walks through it?

These are the questions we will attempt to reflect on when speaking of the birth of the true self and the nature of contemplative union with God. But first we must turn our attention to the true self as it manifests itself in the context of our social dealings with others.

2. The True Self in the World

The world is the place where we meet God because it is the place where God meets us in the person of Jesus Christ. Christ did not merely inhabit human flesh; he became flesh. He made himself, as God, to be one with humanity in the concrete, historical realities of human life. Truly, God has entered into the world and it is in the world that Christians must turn to find God.

But the world is also a place of evil. The world, though punished by a raging flood and purged with fire from heaven, is still the place that stones the prophets, crucifies Christ, and will continue to persecute and malign Christ's followers until the end of time. There is, therefore, an ambivalence inherent in the term "the world." It is the place to which Christ came, the place that God so loved as to send his only begotten Son (Jn 3:16). Yet, at the same time, it is the place that is blind to Christ, that "received him not." It is the place that Satan offered to Jesus if only Jesus would fall down and worship him.

It is this ambivalence of the world that calls for a Christian to be "in the world but not of it." A Christian must love the world, exist in the world as the place God loves, but at the same time reject those aspects of the world that represent an unthinking and communal rejection of God. That is to say, the Christian must reject those aspects of the world that are the communal expressions of the false self.

In our reflections on the true self in the world, we will begin by reflecting upon the world as the place where one finds God in and through simple daily experiences and contact with others. The false self often rejects this world under the guise of "spirituality" and the seeking of invisible realities in other "more spiritual" realms. Merton writes of the folly of all such attempts:

> Very often, the inertia and repugnance which characterize the so-called "spiritual life" of many Christians could perhaps be cured by a simple respect for the concrete realities of everyday life, for nature, for the body, for one's work, one's friends, one's surroundings, etc. A false super-naturalism, which imagines that "the supernatural" is a kind of Platonic realm of abstract essences totally apart from and opposed to the concrete world of nature, offers no real support to a genuine life of meditation and prayer. Meditation has no point and no reality unless it is firmly rooted in *life*. Without such roots, it can produce nothing but the ashen fruits of disgust, *acedia,* and even morbid and degenerate introversion.[1]

The spiritual is that which is ordered toward God. In contrast to this, the unspiritual, degenerate and ashen fruits of the false self consist of that which is intent upon the deification of the ego and the consequent rejection of God's world. Merton was always very careful not to divide the spiritual and the unspiritual into the visible and invisible. An attempt to concentrate on the obtaining of a vision of invisible things may, in fact, be a demonic undertaking.

God is He Who Is and his world is the world that is. What are extraordinary are the ordinary, concrete realities of daily life. And it is our desire to be extraordinary that, in fact, makes us less than ordinary whenever such desires move us to pull away from, reject or even just ignore God manifesting himself to us in the next hot August afternoon or the cold wind of a winter evening.

This basic truth about life in the world becomes all the more important in our social dealings with others:

> From the moment you put a piece of bread in your mouth you are part of the world. . . . Who made the bread? Where did it come from? You are in relationship to the guy who made this stuff. And what is your relationship to him? Do you deserve to be eating this stuff . . . do you have a right to it? That is the world and that is no illusion.[2]

Contemplation may well carry a person off into realms unknown. God surely is "Other" and his otherness allures us and calls us to an ineffable communion with him. Likewise, our true self is more than any of the roles we might happen to play in society. But the point is that all this does not threaten or annihilate our concrete, daily dealings with others, but rather confirms these daily relationships and commitments and establishes them in their proper domain.

Such relationships are harbingers of the false self only when I am led to believe that I am nothing but the sum total of these relationships. In other words, when I begin to believe that the very ground of my identity is derived *solely* from what I do in and through my role in society.

But here the opposite danger must also be seen. In other words, the false self is also exemplified in any escapist mentality that would have us eat our bread and not concern ourselves with our obligations toward those who labored to produce it. One face of the false self smilingly calls upon us to withdraw from our concerns for others and the concrete realities of daily life. The other face of the false self enticingly calls upon us to make a fetish of these commitments, to circle around them with great anxiety like moths around a flame.

The world of productivity and social intercourse is basically good. It is a place I am "in" the moment I put bread in my mouth. I must contribute to it if I am to be true to God, myself and others.

The point is, however, that my contribution must remain an essentially qualitative one. *Who* I am must never be prostituted to the demands of what others tell me I must *do*. Without this basic priority I am reduced to a commodity and I can do little to foster society's half-hidden yet essential purpose of leading its members to full actualization as created persons.

This reveals an important aspect of the vocation of the mystic or the contemplative within the human family. In a sense, the contribution of the contemplative lies in the fact that the contemplative does not make a contribution in the sense the world understands by that word. Merton writes,

> In a certain sense he (the monk) is supposed to be "useless" because his mission is not to *do* this or that job but to *be* a man of God. He does not live in order to exercise a specific function: his business is life itself.[3]

This not only applies to *ex professo* contemplatives living in monasteries. It applies to all Christians living a life of prayer. In prayer we are "useless." We do not "do" anything, but rather open ourselves to be the person God calls us to be. The Moslems say, "God does nothing and therefore there is nothing God does not do." God is beyond pragmatic functions. He is useless, yet by that very fact does all things.

Since we are like God, in our depths we are useless also. So, too, are children and sunsets and the simple recognition of the song of a bird. Death is useless, and so is a simple glance of love. Life itself is useless, for life is to be lived and not ridden in, eaten, packaged, sold or patented. The self in us that prays is useless and it is prayer that allows us to discover the positive uselessness of life in God.

It is likewise a blindness to prayer that exposes us to the pitfalls of becoming ourselves like those,

> . . . for whom a tree has no reality until they think of cutting it down, for whom an animal has no value until it enters a slaughterhouse, men who never look at anything until they decide to abuse it and who never even notice what they do not want to destroy.[4]

This is the lowest kind of love, the love which destroys its object as the love is fulfilled. This is the love of the false self that can appreciate and acknowledge only that which it devours to feed and to foster its own frail shadow existence.

But the contemplative is not useful in the sense which the world is able to understand. By remaining faithful to this uselessness, however, the person of prayer brings to the world that qualitative dimension which saves human life from being but a package that each generation continues to wrap in more cleverly devised slogans and projects.

The combination of Merton's life in the hermitage and his growing concern for the problems of the world appears as an enigma to many. There were those in the monastery who could not understand his concern for world-ly things. On one occasion when I came in to see him, he was downcast because the censors of the Order had just rejected those parts of his *Seeds of Destruction* dealing with atomic warfare. He complained to me, half jokingly, half seriously: "How can I call it *Seeds of Destruction* if they make me take out the destruction?" At the same time many of those in the world could easily relate to what he was saying about social concerns but they could not grasp why he lived in a monastery cut off from the world.

The answer to both sides lies in the paradox that in solitude he rediscovered the heart of the world. It is the paradox that true solitude draws us into communion with others and true communion with others draws us to solitude. His vocation was to find others in solitude. The vocation of people in the world is to find solitude in the midst of others. The true self embraces both solitude and others. The false self rejects both solitude and others. It turns solitude into ego-centered isolation, and communion with others into the mindless "mass man" that feeds on exploi-tation and the externalization of consciousness.

The vision of the true self which we eventually hope to achieve by virtue of our reflections here is a vision which overcomes this polarity and division. Whether in solitude or with others we are called upon to find God, and in find-ing God to find ourselves and others. Plunged in the deepest of solitudes, we find that there are no others "out there," but that there is only the Person in the unity of perfect love which is God. This perfect love rejects nothing that is of God and embraces all things without going anywhere.

II

We take a giant step closer to understanding the place of the world in Merton's spirituality when we begin to

appreciate what it means to say that we and the world interpenetrate, that we are in the world like salt in the ocean.
Merton writes,

> The way to find the real "world" is not merely to
> measure and observe what is outside us, but to dis-
> cover our own inner ground. For that is where
> the world is, first of all: in my deepest self. . . .
> This "ground," this "world" where I am myste-
> riously present at once to my own self and to the
> freedoms of all other men, is not a visible, objec-
> tive and determined structure with fixed laws and
> demands. It is a living and self-creating mystery
> of which I am myself a part, to which I am myself
> my own unique door.[5]

In other words, the world is not "out there" to be
accepted or rejected. An aspect of this interpenetration of
ourselves and the world was seen in the above reference to
our interdependence on one another arising from the goods
we consume and produce. When I eat the bread my brother
made, I am somehow interpenetrated by my brother's toil.
And he in turn is interpenetrated by whatever recompense
I give him in return. As we saw above, this interpenetration
into one another's needs and labors is itself interpenetrated
by God. That is, we cannot reject our brother in need and
claim to have an intimate relationship with God. This
truth is basic to Christian life. Jesus himself told us, "as
often as you did it for one of my least brothers, you did it
for me" (Mt 25:40).

The false self, encased in the hard shell of egocentric
awareness, rejects all such interpenetration with God (with
whom our true self is bound in a union which is our own
ultimate identity) and with others (with whom our true
self is bound in a union of perfect charity). Thus, the false
self is found in a fragmented state which it seeks to over-

come by adherence to the chimera of social myths. By way of social myths the false self is projected into the communal lie of the world, understood in the negative sense as that place which fosters our own deepest lie about ourselves:

> The mother of all lies is the lie we persist in telling ourselves about ourselves. And since we are not brazen enough liars to make ourselves believe our own lie individually, we pool all our lies together and believe them because they have become the big lie uttered by the *vox populi,* and this kind of lie we accept as ultimate truth.[6]

By way of social myths the false self is allowed to surface in concrete expressions of diversion and exploitation. This dark camaraderie coalesces and hardens in a wall that separates ourselves from ourselves, from God and others.

This occurs whenever society makes a cult of some relative interpretation of life or sets some relative good up as the end of life itself. Success, progress, and all similar goals are examples of the world's expression of the false self. These social imperatives hold themselves up as absolutes to the extent that we are led to believe that life is nothing but these things. And in this exclusiveness is the falsity. We are led to believe that only the world can save us. We are told that irrelevance according to the criterion of the world is tantamount to nonexistence. We are what we are to the world and all else is nonbeing.

This is the world that we must leave in order to follow Christ. This is the world Satan showed to Christ in the desert. Satan is the father of this world for he is the father of lies. Thus, to say we are nothing but what the world makes us to be, that the world alone creates us and sustains us, is surely the great lie of Satan contained in the smiling *vox populi.*

For Merton, the all-embracing tentacles of social

myths must be transcended if we are ever to be free, and therefore able to love and be with our brothers and sisters in Spirit and in truth. For Merton, this is one of the important principles of Christian solitude by which we maintain our integrity and wholeness as a created person. Merton tells us that the true solitary is one who:

> . . . realizes, though perhaps confusedly, that he has entered into a *solitude that is really shared by everyone*. . . . What the solitary renounces is not his union with other men, but rather the deceptive fictions and inadequate symbols which tend to take the place of genuine social unity. . . . He (the solitary) realizes that he is one with them in the peril and anguish of their common solitude: not the solitude of the individual only, but the radical and essential solitude of man—a solitude which was assumed by Christ and which, in Christ, becomes mysteriously identified with the solitude of God.[7]

We pray not to recharge our batteries for the business of getting back to the concerns of daily life, but rather to be transformed by God so that the myths and fictions of our life might fall like broken shackles from our wrists. We withdraw within not to retreat from life but to retreat from the constant evasion, the constant fearsome retreat from all that is real in the eyes of God.

The desert where prayer flourishes is the desert of our own hearts barren of all the slogans that we have been led to believe to be our very identity and salvation. Prayer is a death to every identity that does not come from God. And this is why prayer frees us and restores us to ourselves. In prayer we learn from God how to "hate our father and mother" who, through the cult of myth and symbol, represent the world standing before us as the sole source of our identity. And in prayer we learn as well to love our father and mother with a pure heart. In prayer we learn to weep over Jerusalem, love it, walk its streets, hold its children in our laps, even die for it without one word of complaint. But in prayer we also learn that we have a bread of which Jerusalem knows not. We learn that to love Jerusalem is one thing; to prostitute ourselves to it is another. And deeper yet, we learn that we ourselves are Jerusalem. We are Jerusalem redeemed. With Christ we weep over ourselves in our failure to respond to his call. And with Christ we find ourselves forgiven and restored to life through the power of his cross.

And in this is the significance of what was said earlier. We and the world interpenetrate. We are in the world like salt in the ocean. I myself am my own unique door to the world and in a sense the world is the door to myself. A simple walk beneath the trees, a child in need, my obligations to those who labor to make my bread, all these things should lead me to my true self and hence to God.

I am a member of society, of my particular culture which has so saturated me, like oil in a cloth, that a "me" born in another time and place is inconceivable. Birth, love, death and all such life realities have, through my culture, been given a particular meaning. I myself have been given an identity, a role to play, a way of understanding myself and others.

But the most I can do for the world is to transcend it so as to serve it as a person instead of a slave. The only genuine way to serve it is to follow God's will, in which alone the world finds its validity. And, an important expression of God's will is fidelity to some degree of prayer in which I discover and actualize a transcendent self grounded in love.

III

What happens when we wholeheartedly accept the world as teacher and identity giver? What dynamic is set into motion the moment I believe that I will never be anything but what the world tells me I am, and hence believe that the key to being real is always to *adjust* to the demands of society?

> "Trying to adjust" involves a whole galaxy of illusions.

> First of all you take yourself very seriously as an individual, autonomous self, a little isolated world of reality, something quite definitive, something established in its own right: the thinking subject. . . .

> This thinking reality sets itself to consider what is all around it, to get everything in focus. Clear ideas. Clear ideas of *what?* Don't ask too many embarrassing questions, please! What is important is to establish that A is A, and that ten minutes from now it will still be A and a hundred years from now . . . already one has to start adjusting. A hundred years from now A will have vanished forever but the *statement* A is A will be true, adjusted of course to read A *was* A. Then you might have to adjust it to read that at least you thought A was A. However, since you yourself are no longer around, and nobody cares what you thought anyway. . . .[8]

This text provides us with an insight into a very common expression of the false self in the world. The process begins with the individual imagining itself to be a little walled-in existence cut off from, yet living with, countless other little walled-in existences that pool together to form society.

The primary goal of this little walled-in existence that I imagine myself to be is that of adjusting to the demands of society. This is essential, for this little self derives its total meaning (called relevance) from the myths held by the other selves. As the other selves keep changing, adjusting and readjusting these myths, the isolated individual must keep pace in order to avoid falling into nonexistence.

Merton points out that the problem is that this flow of change is moving everyone toward inevitable extinction. The knowers will die. All that was known will be lost or rearranged and offered to new generations of experts who will hold up as new that which is old many times over.

Each society suffers from a we-have-finally-arrived syndrome in which the attitudes, achievements and opinions held by that society are given a colossal significance that towers over what other societies say, think and do. This is not to say our own society, for example, has not made real progress but rather that the whole concept of progress itself is given such top priority that we find it difficult to understand so-called "backward" countries that do not accept it.

The first map makers were known to have placed their own country at the center of the world. Each country still does the same today. And the individuals in each society are expected to believe in and support what the society determines to be significant. To fail to do this is to become oneself insignificant. And in this context not to be significant to the society is not to be at all.

For Merton, one of the primary tasks of all the authentic religious traditions is that of freeing us precisely from this kind of tyranny in which the world is a place that makes absolute demands to which we must comply in order to remain real. Applying this to Merton's own monastic tradition, Merton could, of course, point to the monk as the marginal person *par excellence* who is freed from the ungodly demands of the world.

Merton says of himself that this world is precisely what he left in entering the monastery:

> . . . what do you mean by "the world" anyway? . . . . My concrete answer is: what did I leave when I entered the monastery? As far as I can see, what I abandoned when I "left the world" and came to the monastery was the *understanding of myself* that I had developed in the context of civil society—my identification with what appeared to me to be its aims . . . "the world" . . . did mean a certain set of servitudes that I could no longer accept. . . . Many of these were trivial; some of them were onerous; all are closely related. The image of society that is happy because it drinks Coca-Cola or Seagram's or both and is protected by the bomb.[9]

The prophetic dimension of the contemplative's role (or nonrole) in society is to a great extent grounded in the contemplative's refusal to embrace the world as a god that gives meaning to life without first accepting and receiving life from God. The contemplative, the prophet, is thus for Merton the marginal person, of whom he writes:

> He does not belong to an establishment. He is a marginal person who withdraws deliberately to the margin of society with a view to deepening fundamental human experience. . . . We (marginal people) are deliberately irrelevant. We live with an ingrained irrelevance which is proper to every human being. The marginal man accepts the basic irrelevance of the human condition, an irrelevance which is manifested above all by the fact of death. The marginal person, the monk, the displaced person, the prisoner, all these people live in the presence of death, which calls into question the meaning of life.[10]

Merton points out that this does not produce despair, but hope. He continues:

> . . . we are called by the voice of God, by the voice of that ultimate being, to pierce through the irrelevance of our life, while accepting and admitting that our life is totally irrelevant, in order to find relevance in Him. And this relevance in Him is not something we can grasp or possess. It is something that can only be received as a gift.[11]

The willingness to live in the face of death is essential for the contemplative. Without this exposure to death in order to find life in death the contemplative in this prophetic, marginal stance becomes but another embodiment of the false self, which at one time Merton accuses himself of representing.

> . . . I have myself become a sort of stereotype of the world-denying contemplative—the man who spurned New York, spat on Chicago and tromped on Louisville, heading for the woods with Thoreau in one pocket, John of the Cross in the other, and holding the Bible open to the Apocalypse.[12]

It may be true that every prophet is a pain in the neck, but it is not true that every pain in the neck is a prophet. There is a no more firmly entrenched expression of the false self than the self-proclaimed prophet. He is one who does not die to self but affirms himself in his prophetic criticisms. He is a world unto himself and rare is the person that can measure up to his standards.

We will conclude this section by presenting two incidents taken from monastic life that will help illustrate the sense in which religion should deliver us from the world, but can easily become itself the world in religious garb.

While I was at Gethsemani there was a very old monk

who each year requested the abbot to announce his various anniversaries to the whole community. As the abbot would make the announcement to the assembled community, the old monk would stand and make a slow and solemn bow acknowledging the monks' recognition of his many years in the monastery.

Merton was very good at giving impromptu impersonations of some of the more colorful members of the community. And so on one occasion I asked Merton about this old monk, hoping for a little acted-out characterization. Instead, Merton told me that the monk in question was a holy man, but that I myself would do well to realize that all forms of taking pride in ourselves have a dangerous potential in the spiritual life. He said of himself, "If I make anything out of the fact that I am Thomas Merton, I am dead." And then he added: "And if you make anything out of the fact that you are in charge of the pig barn (a dubious distinction which I had recently received and which I considered to involve some kind of promotion in status) you are dead. The moment you make anything out of anything you are dead."

The lesson here for me was that one sure way to be numbered among the dead would be to set out on a ruthless campaign never to make anything out of anything. The tragic irony of such an endeavor is that, should one succeed, one becomes someone who makes something out of the fact that he never makes anything out of anything! This maze suspiciously resembles the dilemma of the humble person who becomes proud about being humble. The solution Merton suggests is that we should quit keeping score altogether and surrender ourselves with all our sinfulness to God who sees neither the score nor the scorekeeper but only his child redeemed by Christ.

On another occasion I came in to see Merton as he was sorting through some calligraphy prints he had just finished. He explained to me that each one took only a couple of seconds to make: coming directly from the unconscious, one or two sweeps of the brush, without any interference from the conscious mind, produced the desired results. He went through the prints with me and we discussed what he considered to be the more significant points of each. Then he added that the only thing he had any serious doubt about was the small "TM" in the bottom corner of each print. These initials he said were the only alien element in an otherwise spontaneous manifestation of the unconscious mind. Besides that, he added, many people will buy the prints, whether they are good or not, "simply because of those two letters which stand for someone who does not even exist."

Fame and success are the myth of the ego taken root like an acorn in the soil of the world. The myth assumes gigantic proportions. On this point Merton tells us of an occasion in his own life:

> A few years ago a man who was compiling a book on Success wrote and asked me to contribute a statement on how I got to be a success. I replied indignantly that I was not able to consider myself a success in any terms that had a meaning to me. I swore I had spent my life strenuously avoiding success. If it happened that I had once written a best-seller this was a pure accident, due to inattention and naivete, and I would take very good care never to do the same thing again. If I had a message to my contemporaries, I said, it was surely this: be anything you like, be madmen, drunks, and bastards of every shape and form, but at all costs avoid one thing: success. I heard no more from him, and I am not aware that my reply was published with the other testimonials.[13]

What is being said here does not add up to a condemnation of success but rather to a warning against what is implied in the *cult,* the fascination, the restless drive for success. By success we become somebody and cling to this somebody who exists only in the mirrored reflection in the eyes of our admirers. This somebody was first glimpsed in the eyes of Adam and Eve as they saw themselves reflected in the eyes of their altogether too naked partner. It is the somebody that is rich for having made something out of something; that is, for having taken a relative truth and clinging to it as an absolute source of an imagined identity. Yet this very wealth is this somebody's poverty, the ontological poverty of being cut off from God as the only source of the human heart's fulfillment.

It is this somebody who dies in prayer and, having died, leaves us liberated to receive our true glory and our true fulfillment which comes to us from the hands of God. Surely, not to acknowledge the good we have done is but the reverse image of clinging to success as a source of ultimate identity. Both the craving for and the rejection of success are expressions of the false self which is false precisely because it fails to see things as they are.

In prayer we come before God, and in silence are cleansed of all such imaginary claims. We come with no money with which to buy God's wares. And in our poverty he tells us that we have no need of money, for although we have nothing we are the heirs of everything. We possess in him the pearl of great price which is our own self as one with him in love. While empty we are filled. While poor we possess that Kingdom of which no one but God can know the boundaries, for its boundaries are one with God's own infinite life, which he gives to us as persons redeemed by Christ.

IV

What do we do when the world threatens to rob us of our own essential integrity before God? What can be the solution to such an all-embracing illusion? How are we to be freed from it? Merton answers by saying:

> The cross is the great Christian answer to the world as a problem. The cross is liberation. The cross is the only liberation from the servitude to the illusions which are packaged and sold as the world . . . the cross transforms the world . . . and once the cross has been accepted fully in our life then we can begin to make sense about this whole entity, the world.[14]

But what does it mean to allow the cross to be fully accepted in our lives? The cross is where Christ gained all by losing all. It is where, as Paul says, Christ ". . . did not deem equality with God something to be grasped at. Rather, he emptied himself and took the form of a slave, being born in the likeness of men" (Phil 2:6-7).

Jesus took the world upon himself. He became flesh and in his death he healed flesh and redeemed it. He interpenetrated himself with our collective weakness. He allowed himself to be engulfed by it, brought to nothing, poured out into an emptiness from which he rose victorious, calling us to share in his cross that we might share in his eternal life.

Thus, by accepting the cross in our lives we come to accept our falsity as healed. And we come to yield to the Spirit's action in us, the Spirit who draws us to die with Christ that we might rise with him. Merton writes:

> Once we have accepted the cross . . . then we become able to realize that the world is in our-

selves and the world in ourselves is good and redeemed. And we can accept in ourselves both the evil and the good which are in us and in everybody else and which go to make up the world. . . . We are the world . . . but we are it as redeemed. Then we see right away that the world is a question of interpenetration.[15]

The spiritual life is the life of Christ living in us. And Christ is God who has interpenetrated all our falsity and claimed our weakness as his own. It is in our death to self, understood as our participation in the death of Christ, that we realize that the question of choosing the world or choosing Christ is, in fact, a completely misguided question:

> Do we really choose between the world and Christ as between two conflicting realities absolutely opposed? Or do we choose Christ by choosing the world as it really is in him, that is to say created and redeemed by him, and encountered in the ground of our own personal freedom and of our love? Do we really renounce ourselves and the world in order to find Christ, or do we renounce our alienated and false selves in order to choose our own deepest truth in choosing both the world and Christ at the same time? If the deepest ground of my being is love, then in that very love itself and nowhere else will I find myself, and the world, and my brother and Christ. It is not a question of either-or but of all-in-one . . . of wholeness, wholeheartedness and unity . . . which finds the same ground of love in everything.[16]

In prayer we hang upon the cross with the thief at Christ's right side. As Christ hangs dying we hear him tell us, "This day you will be with me in Paradise." Suddenly in the midst of all our thievery and pain, Christ's cross becomes our own and we discover that his death becomes our life. By taking the cross of Christ upon us there is no longer a world out there to reject, nor is there a world within to reject. There is no dualistic opposition of any kind. We find that the world as an enemy disappears in an all-in-one wholeness in which we are recreated in the redeeming love of Christ. Our prayer and our life become our yes to this saving wholeness.

In Christ is found the hidden wholeness that binds together as one all we call the world, with all we ourselves are. Christ, his arms at once extended on the cross and uplifted in glory, embraces all that is weak, leaves it weak yet fills it with power. He leaves it sinful and poor, yet raises it up before the gaze of the Father who sees not our weakness but his Son.

3. The True Self in Religious Searching

I

As Dietrich Bonhoeffer sat in prison awaiting his execution by the Nazis he wrote on the now almost proverbial theme of the need for religionless Christianity. He observed that if Saint Paul could ask, "Can we not be saved without the Law?" should we not now ask, "Can we not be saved without religion?" The reason for his question is not difficult to find. While the smell of human flesh was in the air, the churchmen of his day were preaching on spiritual matters. Their silence about Hitler's atrocities spoke louder than words as to the impotency of religion as a vital expression of God's action upon the world.

Bonhoeffer's insights gave contemporary expression to something we have always known to be true; namely, that under the banner of religion men and women can stray far from God. Religion takes us not only into heaven. It also takes us into insane asylums and battlefields. It also leads us to walk a wide circle around the Samaritan lying half-dead in the ditch or around the child in the ghetto.

In Jesus' day it was the religious people, the Pharisees, and not the prostitutes and tax collectors, to whom Jesus

59

directed his most caustic accusations. And it was the whited sepulchers, the religious people, who had Jesus put to death. Of course, being religious they felt no guilt for what they did because they did it in the name of God.

It is little wonder then that the term "religious" is often a pejorative one indicating an escapist, self-righteous, other-worldly or perhaps superstitious stance toward life. Nor should this come as any surprise, in light of all we have been saying of the pervasiveness of the false self. Since religion deals with the ultimate realities of life, it is under-standable that religion would draw out the ultimate in the false self's basic disorientation and blindness. The false self can have but false gods, all of which in the end turn out to be but reflections of the false self as it worships itself and sets itself up as the reason for its own existence.

All these and similar forms of religious thought and action must be seen as standing in sharp contrast to au-thentic religious expression, which stands as the highest expression of human awareness and desire. This becomes clear in reference to Merton. His writings are sometimes philosophical or theological, sometimes poetic or anthropo-logical, but they are always religious. Indeed, his whole life was fundamentally religious. That is to say, all his actions, talents and ambitions were finally focused solely upon the goal of achieving transforming union with God. As he expressed it:

> Whatever I may have written, I think it can all be reduced in the end to this one root truth: That God calls human persons to union with Himself with one another in Christ.[1]

We can say that, for Merton, religion refers to our deepest reality which lies hidden in our innate propensity for union with God. Our life, in other words, simply makes no sense whatsoever except to the extent it is directed toward union with God, that is, to the extent that it is authentically religious.

The following words by Johannes B. Metz will help to clarify the full dimensions of religion as a manifestation of man's deepest reality:

> If man leaves his dreamy conceptions aside and focuses on his naked poverty, when the masks fall away and the core of his Being is revealed, it soon becomes obvious that he is religious "by nature," that religion is the secret dowry of his being. In the midst of his existence there unfolds the bond (*re-ligio*) which ties him to the infinitely transcendent mystery of God, the insatiable interest in the Absolute that captivates him and underlines his poverty.

> At the core of his existence a "transcendental neediness" holds sway. It spurs and supports all his longings and desires, works itself out through them, but is never exhausted in them.[2]

Metz's words echo Augustine's, "You made our hearts for thee, O Lord, and our hearts are restless until they rest in thee." It is obvious that religion, thus understood, is in no way an appendage or a culturally imposed superstructure added to our being, but is rather a manifestation of his deepest reality. For religious man, life is essentially a journey in which one sets out to quench a thirst, not simply to know that a God exists but to drink directly from God's own life to which man is bonded (*re-ligio*) in the depths of his being. Religion is thus the intuitively known and symbolically expressed desire to become who we are in God. The fulfilling of this desire is the realization of the true self.

The religious life moves in two directions that are

ultimately revealed as one. There is a vertical direction which arises from the root awareness of a bond with transcendence, as described by Metz. There is also a horizontal direction arising from the fact that we do not go to God in isolation from others but only with others as our brothers and sisters. And underlying both the vertical and horizontal directions of religious experience there is the paradox that in Christ the horizontal and vertical meet and become one.

In realizing that union with God is achieved in and through union with others we see that the religious person is basically a loving person. He loves others not simply out of personal inclination or an arbitrary external law, but rather because he intuits God's presence in the presence of the other. In the golden rule is found a touchstone with God. In the "nearest Thou at hand" is found the eternal. Selfless love for others sets the religious person free, restores him to himself, as he gives himself in compassion and concern.

But the awareness of the necessity of loving others does not bring with it the strength to do so, and in this is found a basic expression of the poverty of religious man. We are made for God and grow in union with him in and through our loving union with others, yet in the face of this we still find ourselves filled with selfishness. We discover a wound deep within us. We bear the weight of an ontological disorientation, a frightful inability to root out the death-dealing narcissism that impregnates our being, making our best intentions impotent. And so the religious man cries out for help. He intuits and experiences his poverty in which he lacks the light and strength to be of himself a child of God.

Jesus is God's answer to our cry. The believing Christian knows that while he stands alone he can do nothing, yet he is filled with hope for he knows that the self that stands alone is no more. Christ has come. He has identified himself with us forever. He has transformed us from within, loving our weakness and, through his cross, making our weakness our strength.

Jesus gives us the Spirit and so makes us one with God. This gift reveals the deeper dimensions of our love for others and empowers us to reach these dimensions. It is the Spirit that allows us to see that to love another is to love Christ.

Christ has identified himself with the human family, especially the poor and the forgotten. In loving them we love him in them. And they, in turn, encounter him in us in the love we give them. And in this the bonds of charity are formed, building up one Christ unto the eternal glory of the Father.

In Merton we find these basic characteristics of the merger of the vertical and the horizontal dimensions of religious experience and response. For example, he writes:

> But indeed we exist solely for this, to be the place He has chosen for His presence, His manifestation in the world, His epiphany. . . . The love of our fellow man is given us as the way of realizing this. . . . It is the love of my lover, my brother, or my child that sees God in me, makes God credible to myself in me. And it is my love for my lover, my child, my brother that enables me to show God to him or her in himself or herself. Love is the epiphany of God in our poverty.[3]

Merton assumed that authentic religious experience constantly challenges us to live up to the concrete daily demands of love as incarnated in our brothers and sisters in need. The foundation of this love is Christ who fills our humanity with God's own life. Just as Christ loves us with the same love with which he loves the Father, so too are we to love others with the same love with which we love God.

It is the Spirit within that enables us to see that, "It is not a matter of *either* God *or* man, but of finding God by loving man, and discovering the true meaning of man in our love for God."[4] Love for God and love for others are not two loves, but rather two manifestations of one love. These two manifestations are bound so closely to each other that one is impossible without the other. As strongly as Merton stresses the reality and importance of love for God in contemplative prayer, he no less stresses the fundamental fact of the spiritual life that:

> A man cannot enter into the deepest center of himself and pass through that center into God, unless he is able to pass entirely out of himself and empty himself and give himself to other people in the purity of a selfless love.[5]

Merton once told me that prayer must make us more sensitive to the plight of others. He said, "as long as one person suffers, you suffer, too. It must be so or your prayer is of little value." Saint Paul's, "I fill up what is lacking in the suffering Christ" is closely attuned to these words of Merton. It is so easy to misinterpret talk of ecstasy, of self beyond self, mystical union, or such similar expressions as implying a kind of distance between our inner self and the daily simple problems of others. In a sense this is so. There is a distance proper to prayer. We go off and pray in secret. We go off alone. We go off, leaving even ourselves as we normally conceive of ourselves. But this distance is for the sake of union. Solitude, if it is genuine, brings us to a most profound communion with others in their deepest reality grounded in God.

A helpful image in understanding the monastic notion of solitude and union with others is that of a large group of people formed in a circle. As each individual in the circle simultaneously begins to walk slowly toward the center of the circle, he or she discovers that all are inevitably drawing closer to one another. Physically it is impossible for them all to stand at once in the precise center. But in prayer this is possible. Christ is that center and, as we go out of ourselves into him in solitary prayer we go out of ourselves into the most real dimension of others—not the individual, circumscribable, empirical self that changes and shifts like clouds in a storm, but rather the true self, the self grounded in the love of God.

In the cross of Jesus the vertical and the horizontal become one. In a touch of compassion Christ touches Christ. In a moment of solitary union with God we arrive at the center which is hidden, yet everywhere, and from which all of humanity, knowingly or unknowingly, cries out for and receives the healing touch of God. In prayer, one with Christ, we hold everyone in our hearts and the secret longings of all become our own.

Our union with others is essential to our union with God, and our union with God is essential to our union with others. Neither one supersedes the other; rather, each presupposes the other. Each one properly pursued leads to the other.

If Christian service is authentic, it gradually deepens our desire to see directly the face of God reflected in the faces of our brothers and sisters. We become more and more imbued with the yearnings of the psalmist who cried out, "O God, you are my God whom I seek; for you my flesh pines and my soul thirsts like the earth, parched, lifeless and without water" (Ps 63:1).

Christ served many people in many ways. Yet his greatest service, his greatest sign of power this side of death, was his death itself. Helplessly nailed to the cross, he saved us by handing himself over to the Father. Prayer is a vital expression of our share in this handing over, this deliverance, this passing over from death to life. Surely, central to the gospel is the truth that Christ came not only to unite us to one another but to take us in the Spirit to the Father. In prayer is found the ground of service, the ultimate *why* behind the truth that to help another is to draw closer to Christ.

Father Daniel Walsh, Merton's lifelong mentor and friend, expressed the relationship between prayer and service by saying, "most are called to salvation primarily through witnessing to *God in man* by loving service to others. The contemplative, while in no way exempt from loving service, finds salvation primarily through witnessing to *man in God* by a life of fidelity to contemplative prayer." The vision of the contemplative is a vision of perfect unity beyond all division, including any kind of pseudodivision between prayer and service. The degree of witness in each person's life is a matter of charism. Both selfless love and prayer reveal the true self. Both selfless love and prayer unmask the false self. Both prayer and service therefore are the proper domain of the religious person and it is the religious person that recognizes in both their ultimate validity and worth as well as the ultimate self they express and actualize.

II

We saw in a previous chapter how, after Adam passed through the center of self, putting himself between himself and God, he immediately began to reconstruct the universe in his own image and likeness. Lacking God's power to create tangible things, the false self creates by use of ideologies, definitions, social myths and words. The false self gives its own name to life and then, like a self-proclaimed demiurge, demands that all of life conform to its wishes.

What is enacted here is the tragic error of naming the elephant and then trying to ride home on the name given, instead of on the elephant itself.

This whole process frequently occurs in religion as well. We give God a name. We then equate God with the name we have given him, and in doing so we make ourselves, in effect, God's God. Instead of acknowledging God as the source of our identity and existence, we make ourselves the self-proclaimed source of God's identity. God then becomes the one made in our image and likeness.

Those engaged in the undertaking of naming God see themselves to be participating in a holy work. They are the God-definers, the definition makers. They give shape to the ultimate perimeters of life.

Of course, one of the procedural principles is that God is everything and we are nothing. But they define what this means. They mark off those who properly grasp it from those who do not. Thus, while maintaining that they are nothing, they turn their nothing into a nothing that defines itself and thereby make that nothingness into a kind of everything to which all who wish to know the truth must listen. This is a far cry from the true theological inquiry but it is not a far cry from the stance of the Pharisee who is always with us in the form of a deep-seated universal tendency within ourselves. It is the false self expressing its futile, odious outcry against the Creative sovereignty of the divine freedom.

Merton's insights into this aspect of the false self begin once again with the self seen as the isolated unit of the ego:

> . . . considering himself as a completely autonomous unit all on his own. . . . He is the boss of his life . . . stranded in the midst of everything, and he has got to make sense of it. . . . He

> is all the time at the center. . . . He decides every-
> thing, defended from reality by this little wall
> which constitutes, as he thinks, his individuality.[6]

Once the false self gives birth to its own dark gossamer
existence as cut off from God, it begins to function as its
own God by passing final decisions and judgments upon
everything under the sun. A whole system of formulas,
laws and ideologies is created to form not only one's relationship to others but to God as well. Both self and God
become equated with the definitions given to them. Both
God and self become cogs in a smoothly running system of
self-creation.

Merton points to the futility of this whole process.

> The idea that you can choose yourself, approve
> yourself, and then offer yourself (fully "chosen"
> and "approved") to God, applies the assertion of
> yourself over against God. From this root of
> error comes all the sour leafage and fruitage of a
> life of self-examination, interminable problems
> and unending decisions, always making right
> choices, walking on the razor edge of an impos-
> sibly subtle ethic. . . . All this implies the frenzied
> conviction that one can be his own light and his
> own justification, and that God is there for a pur-
> pose: to issue a stamp of confirmation upon my
> own rightness. In such a religion the Cross be-
> comes meaningless except as the (blasphemous)
> certification that because you suffer, because you
> are misunderstood, you are justified twice over—
> you are a martyr. Martyr means witness. You
> are then a witness. To what? To your own in-
> fallible light and your own justice, which you
> have *chosen*.
> This is the exact opposite of everything
> Jesus ever did or taught.

To unveil the folly of this tendency to pin down and identify God's will with ideologies and moral laws, Merton humorously observes:

> Pontiffs! Pontiffs! We are all pontiffs haranguing one another, brandishing our croziers at one another, dogmatizing, threatening anathemas!

> Recently in the breviary we had a saint who, at the point of death, removed his pontifical vestments *and got out of bed.* He died on the floor, which is only right: but one hardly has time to be edified by it—one it still musing over the fact that he had pontifical vestments on in bed.

> Let us examine our consciences, brethren: do we wear our miters even to bed? I am afraid we sometimes do.[8]

Merton also speaks of the religious life, and more particularly of the monastic life, as falling prey to this frantic exercise of self-defining projects:

> The monastic life as a whole is a hot medium. Hot with words like "must," "ought" and "should." Communities are devoted to high-definition projects: making it all clear. The clearer it gets the more clear it has to be made. It branches out. You have to keep clearing the branches. The more branches you cut back the more branches grow. For one you cut you get three more. On the end of each branch there is a big bushy question mark. People are all running around with big packages of meaning. Each is very anxious to know whether all the others have received the latest messages. Has someone else received a message that he has not received? Will they be willing to pass it on to him? Will he

understand it when it is passed on? Will he have
to argue about it? Will he be expected to clear
his throat and stand up and say. . . "Well, the way
I look at it. . ."?[9]

There is a sad urgency and evasive anxiety at work
here. There is some elusive treasure to protect from we
know not what forces. Prophets are stoned with enthusiasm.
Their last breath is met with a sigh of great relief, for the
one who threatened to pull down the holy object has been
destroyed. And the God beyond the scope of our definitions
and moral, social principles is a God feared to the extent
that even the possibility of his existence is discarded as
irrelevant. This does not mean God is not said to be transcendent. But rather transcendence itself is defined and
thereby removed as a threat.

Merton puts his finger on the tragedy of this whole
endeavor when he says: "Instead of dealing with God we
are dealing with this great system. . . . What we are dealing
with ultimately is ourselves. . . . You are stuck with your-
self and nothing else but!"[10]

The closest a participant in this game can come to
heaven is to look in a mirror. Their God is truly "their
God" in that he is nothing but their definitions of him. And
the way to reach him is nothing but the moral precepts they
themselves have devised.

The notion of worthiness is often prominent in this
expression of religion. And the motivating force behind
much of the principle making is that of having the security
of knowing one is worthy of God. This knowledge is possible because God here is the God who does not go beyond
our definitions. Even when one morally fails (and one
often does fail for the rules set a high standard that calls
for a Titan's effort to maintain even an average score) one
is still left secure. One's worthiness is not really threatened,

for one has also constructed a set of principles defining exactly why one failed. And also a set of principles on exactly how to regain God's graces.

Merton makes very clear that he is in no way attacking the necessity of principles in all areas of human life, including religion. History teaches us that when people recklessly throw off moral and religious principles in order to be "free," they more often than not find themselves hopelessly entangled in the unforeseen repercussions of their narrow-minded enthusiasm. One of the first tasks of any revolution is always that of setting up a new (and hopefully better) set of structures in the form of new laws and principles. Without principles there is chaos. It is holiness alone that frees us to abandon principles as absolutes so as to follow Augustine's adage to "Love and do what you will."

But what Merton is talking about is the absolutizing of a relative good. Instead of principles pointing to a reality, they become the reality itself. Instead of moral laws being norms of behavior they become ironclad verifications of "worthiness."

Merton states that the way out of this error is to realize that,

> God is asking me, the unworthy, to forget my unworthiness and that of my brothers, and dare to advance in the love which has redeemed and renewed us all in God's likeness. And to laugh, after all, at the preposterous idea of "worthiness."[11]

But, of course, the false self is not laughing. It cannot afford to do so, for it has based its entire existence upon itself as an autonomous center that creates itself and God, both of whom are firmly held in place by and identified with its own principles, conformity to which assures worthiness. It *must* be worthy for it has decreed itself to be so.

For Merton the way out of this whole dilemma is that of going back to our most fundamental relationship to God in which both "in life and in death we depend entirely on Him."[12] In realizing our dependency upon him we realize that our task before God is one in which "we submit ourselves entirely to God in order to let him work with us."[13]

Merton makes clear that it is not our sins of weakness that keep us from God. All our sinfulness has been redeemed by Christ. We have but to bring our failings to him with sincere repentance and we find ourselves forgiven. What does endanger our relationship with God, however, is this moralizing attitude we have been discussing here.

Merton asserts the way to break out of the confining prison of any ideology is that of finding God in life itself. Christ has taken on the human condition in its simple concreteness. My very humanity places me in union with God. Therefore, Merton says:

> plain life as lived by a Christian . . . in a spirit of faith, is a life redeemed by Christ. It is Christ's life. . . . When you eat breakfast, Christ is eating breakfast. When you go to work, Christ is going to work. When you meet your brother . . . Christ meets Christ.[14]

In Jesus, God has claimed our life as his own. A simple openness to the next human moment brings us into union with God in Christ. This central truth is the Christocentric expression of our most fundamental relationship to God as creatures. In reference to this point Merton quotes Meister Eckhart as saying, "For God *to be* is to give being, and for man *to be* is to receive being."[15] Our true self is a received self. At each moment we exist to the extent we receive existence from him who is existence.

As indicated earlier, our deepest freedom rests not in our freedom to do what we want to do but rather in our freedom to become who God wills us to be. This person, this ultimate self God wills us to be, is not a predetermined, static mold to which we must conform. Rather, it is an infinite possibility of growth. It is our true self; that is, a secret self hidden in and one with the divine freedom. In obeying God, in turning to do his will, we find him willing us to be free. He created us for freedom; that is to say, he created us for himself.

Phrased differently, we can say that God cannot hear the prayer of someone who does not exist. The self constructed of ideologies and social principles, the self that defines itself and proclaims its own worthiness is most unworthy of the claim to reality before God. Our freedom from the prison of our own illusions comes in realizing that in the end everything is a gift. Above all, we ourselves are gifts that we must first accept before we can become who we are by returning who we are to the Father. This is accomplished in a daily death to self, in a compassionate reaching out to those in need, and in a detached desire for the silent, ineffable surrender of contemplative prayer. It is accomplished in making Jesus' prayer our own: "Father . . . not my will but yours be done."

III

We have just examined one manifestation of how the false self seeks God—through a form of religious expression that keeps its distance from God. In fact, finding God himself would be intolerable, for his infinite freedom would upset the apple cart of the hardened moral principles and theological conclusions so carefully arranged by the false self. Self-proclaimed definitions are as close as the false self cares to get or can afford to get to reality. Merton writes of this kind of religiosity:

> Let them claim that the world has a definite meaning: but that they do not know what the meaning is. Let them claim life has its obligations: but they do not want to find out what they may be. They assert that the gods are all quite real, but they do not want to have anything to do, one way or another, with divinity. Rightness, piety, justice, religion consist, for them, in the definition of various essences.[16]

He calls this group the "right thinking." God never excites them, for they are only excited when one of their definitions is threatened or when they come up with a new definition that especially pleases them.

But there is an opposite approach which the false self can take before God. This approach is referred to by Merton as "Promethean theology." Prometheus, of course, is the mythic figure who stole fire from the gods, was discovered, and was forced to undergo unending torment. Promethean theology is not characteristic of the false self as it is exemplified in the cool reserve of the right thinking, protected from God by layer upon layer of self-devised principles. Rather, in Promethean theology we see the false self risking all in order to taste directly of God's own life. Here the false self does not try to shape its nothingness into something real; instead, because it recognizes its nothingness before God, it tries to steal some share of God's infinite actuality. Merton states that some elements of this mode of the false self are in all of us.

> The Promethean instinct is as deep as man's weakness. That is to say, it is almost infinite. It has its roots in the bottomless abyss of man's own

nothingness. It is the despairing cry that rises out
of the darkness of man's metaphysical solitude—
the inarticulate expression of a terror man will
not admit to himself: his terror at having to be
himself, at having to be a person.[17]

The falsity emerges here not in a false understanding
of what *I* am, for of myself I am truly nothing. The falsity
lies in making God into an infinite false self, an infinite ego
that jealously guards his life against all who would approach.

It is true that we are nothing without God, but the
God who abandons us to our nothingness simply does not
exist. The God who would create us so as to be fulfilled
by him alone, and then punish us for approaching him, is a
God that could only exist in our own perverted imagination.
The self made in the image of such a god can only be a
false self, a self that has to steal God's life while God is not
looking.

One common expression of Promethean theology is
the "save my soul" spirituality, which holds that Christian
life is an effort carried out against unbelievable odds. Christian life is like the struggle of Sisyphus pushing his stone
up the hill. It is God who has made the hill steep. It is
God who sees to it that the stone is heavy. It is God who
makes sure that the stone never reaches the top of the hill.
The fires of God's life merge with the fires of hell which
God supposedly places like a flickering sphinx between
himself and his creatures who dare to approach him. Entrance into heaven is said to be gained by tricking the devil,
by "getting into heaven a half hour before the devil knows
you're dead." In this system salvation is gained only by
tricking God. Our sinfulness places us on a greased pole
going down into hell. But, by a superhuman effort and a
final barrage of highly efficacious prayers, we can manage

to trick God into letting an unwanted sinner into his kingdom.

Promethean man is man aware of the mystery of his solitude: An owl sitting alone in the forest at night is not lonely. The owl is the forest. The blackness of the night is his mother. He preens his feathers, needing no one to observe or comment upon his solitary beauty. But a man alone in the forest at night is lonely indeed. The blackness of the night is not his mother but a mirror of his own solitude—a vast unknown expanse of nothingness which he both carries about within him and stands before like a frightened stranger.

Promethean man has not the superficiality of the right thinking. He intuits the depths of things and in the depths experiences his nothingness. He seeks deliverance and sets out to get it by stealing it from God.

Merton puts his finger on the crux of the problem inherent in this spirituality by saying the error lies in the total misunderstanding of *possession*. Merton writes, "In whatever form it takes, Promethean spirituality is obsessed with 'mine' and 'thine'—on the distinction between what is 'mine' and what belongs to God."[18]

What does not occur to Prometheus is that the life of God is in fact given as a free gift. The very reason God created us in the first place was to share this gift. Yet, for Prometheus, a life freely given is not recognizable as life. Such a freely given gift does not uphold the false self's intrinsic need to own life autonomously. Prometheus sees no share in God's life valid unless he can steal it, unless he can say it is "mine." Merton writes,

> He cannot enjoy the gift of God unless he snatches it away when God is not looking. This is necessary, for Prometheus demands that the fire be his by right or conquest. Otherwise he will not believe it is really his own.[19]

For Prometheus the vision of God's life is his hell. This is so because he does not recognize God's life in himself freely given as a gift. This freely given presence of God is not recognized, for it does not conform to the self in its ego-centered sphere. God can be worshiped only with the secret hope of somehow stealing God's secret and thus in the end being able to worship one's self. As Merton expresses it, "The fire Prometheus steals from the gods is his own incommunicable reality, his own spirit. . . . Yet this being is a gift of God, and it does not have to be stolen. It can only be had by a free gift—the very hope of gaining it by theft is pure illusion."[20]

We find a basic paradox: the experience of twisting in torment on the axis of our own desires while God, the fulfillment of our desires, stands within us as an unnoticed gift freely given. Merton expresses this experience by asking himself,

> Perhaps I am stronger than I think.
>
> Perhaps I am even afraid of my strength, and turn it against myself, thus making myself weak. Making myself secure. Making myself guilty.
>
> Perhaps I am most afraid of the strength of God in me. Perhaps I would rather be guilty and weak in myself, than strong in Him whom I cannot understand.[21]

Merton works from the experience of this paradox into the first realization of how we are to be delivered from it.

> It is a greater thing and a better prayer to live in Him Who is Infinite, and to rejoice that He is Infinite, than to strive always to press His infin-

ity into the narrow space of our own hearts. As long as I am content to know that He is infinitely greater than I, and that I cannot know Him unless He shows Himself to me, I will have Peace, and He will be near me and in me, and I will rest in Him. But as soon as I desire to know and enjoy Him for myself, I reach out to do violence to Him Who evades me, and in so doing I do violence to myself and fall back upon myself in sorrow and anxiety, knowing that He has gone His way.[22]

He says elsewhere that freedom from the futility of Prometheus is in reversing Prometheus' most basic assumptions about ownership and conquest, about laying hold of God as a possession.

Only when we are able to "let go" of everything within us, all desire to see, to know, to taste, and to experience the presence of God, do we truly become able to experience that presence with the overwhelming conviction and reality that revolutionize our entire inner life.[23]

This letting-go in the moral order is the living out of the Beatitudes. In the order of prayer it is in-depth *kenosis,* an emptying out of the contents of awareness so that one becomes oneself an empty vessel, a broken vessel, a void that lies open before God and finds itself filled with God's own life. This gift of God is revealed to be the ground and root of our very existence. It is our own true self.

It is in this awareness that the notions of "mine" and "thine" fall apart. As Merton beautifully expresses it,

. . . *everything is mine* precisely because *everything is His.* If it were not His, it could never be mine. If it could not be mine, He would not even want it for Himself. And all that is His is His very self. All that he gives me becomes, in some

way, my own self. What then is mine? He is
mine. And what is His? I am His.[24]

IV

Merton often bemoaned the widespread mistrust of
mysticism by monks, as well as by those in other walks of
life. Too many no longer even believe in the possibility of
genuine mystical union with God, much less see it as a vital
dimension of the holiness of the Church. Merton would
say that we dare not place any limitation on what is possible in prayer. We dare not waver from the childlike faith
that knows without reserve that all things are possible in
prayer.

It must be pointed out, however, that it is not prayer
we seek in prayer but God himself. It is not an experience
of God we seek but the living God inherent in, yet tran-
scending, all experience. On one occasion Merton brought
this out to me: "The trouble with monastic life is that too
many enter it with the hope of becoming a mystic. What
they do not realize is that in being a mystic you are not
more than you were before, you're less. In fact, there is
nobody left but God."

There is no contemplation without desire. But the
desire proper to contemplation is shadowed by the subtle
surrogate of the false self seeking to assert itself by way of
contemplation. The false self desires to "become a mystic"
in order to establish yet new frontiers to its domain, in order
to stake out yet new claims of victory. The difficulty is that,
at the level of appearances, the true quest for God in prayer
and the effort of the false self to assert itself in prayer are
two pursuits that can be most difficult to distinguish from
each other. This is why the gift of discernment is so
important in the ways of prayer. It is a gift of the Spirit to
discover these two opposite yet look-alike pursuits. By

way of discernment one discovers that, though similar in appearance, one leads to heaven and the other leads to hell. One brings forth the person in God. The other brings forth but illusions and reveals but an isolated figure crouched in the shadows eating a forbidden fruit that turns out to be poison.

The following experience helped me form a concrete image of true and false pursuit of contemplative prayer:

Each Sunday the novices were allowed beyond the enclosure wall to walk in the woods, to read and pray. Merton's hermitage sat on the edge of a rather large clearing atop a wooded hill overlooking some of the low-lying farmland of the monastery.

I was late in getting back from my walk and, in an attempt to save time, thought I would walk across the clearing in front of Merton's hermitage. But before I reached the edge of the clearing I saw Merton sitting in a lotus position a few yards in front of his hermitage. He sat, motionless, his back erect, his eyes closed. I stood in silence and watched him there, Buddha-like, sitting in the grass.

To me at the time it was a powerful, concrete image of all Merton stood for—the existential, living reality of contemplative union with God, the great truth that intimacy with God is a living reality for those who seek it with all their hearts, the great truth that all things are possible for those who pray. Merton, as it were, sat as a transparent opening into God who calls each of us to union with himself.

But within this opening of light and emptiness there emerges the danger of an opaque idol worship. One's own ego, as an idol seeking adoration, projects its dark wishes into another who has really "made it." Within this framework prayer ceases to become a childlike abandonment to God, as spurred on through the witness of another, and becomes instead an esoteric pursuit for an experience that will but widen the prison of ego consciousness to wider mystical perimeters. Under the guise of prayer is a twisted project carried on by someone God knows nothing about.

We must come to our prayer the way a child takes a drink of water. We must sit in prayer in the simplicity with which the reflection of a cloud sets weightlessly upon the surface of some secluded pond. Our prayer is not an identity-giver. It does not embellish or add a single ounce to the weight of the prize-grabbing ego. In fact, says Merton, the opposite is true. The path to union with God

> is a path of ascetic self-emptying and "self-naughting" and not at all a path of self-affirmation, of self-fulfilment or of "perfect attainment."[25]

It is for this reason that any expression of a zealous search for spiritual attainment is most likely to proceed from the false self. It is our false selves which see ourselves as "potential subjects for special and unique experiences, or as candidates for realization, attainment and fulfillment."[26]

Here Merton sees one of the primary roles of a good spiritual director to be that of conducting a "ruthless campaign against all forms of delusion arising out of spiritual ambition and self-complacency which aim to establish the ego in spiritual glory."[27]

It is true that a good spiritual director is hard to find. But it is also true that our real spiritual directors, our real gurus, are our loved ones who place upon us unexplainable burdens, force us to proceed out from our narcissistic prison into a selfless encounter in love. Our gurus are all those places in our hearts at which we stand the risk of losing everything. Our guru is the child within—small and simple and without pretense, who would have us reach out in a tender healing touch without our left hand knowing what our right hand is doing. Our guru is death who teaches us that we gain all by losing all.

V

There is a tremendous fascination today with Eastern spiritualities. As a conclusion to this chapter we will reflect on Merton's insights into the ways in which the pursuit of Eastern meditation techniques is in fact often but expressions of the false self.

The material we are using here appears in *Mystics and Zen Masters* where Merton lists what he calls three wrong attitudes about Eastern meditation. The first wrong attitude is one we have seen before: namely, that we go to meditation as an ego, "an empirical self, an 'I' which, with all the good intentions in the world, sets out to 'achieve liberation.' "[28] The central concern and necessity of this "I" is always to affirm itself; now, by way of meditation, it seeks the ultimate affirmation.

Merton states that the second wrong attitude is that of looking upon the mind as an object to be possessed. The goal of meditation then becomes to discover and seize hold of our own hidden "inner mind." Merton writes,

> Thus the mind is regarded not as something I am but as something I *own*. It then becomes necessary for me to sit quietly and calmly, recollecting my faculties and reaching down to experience my "mind."[29]

Here the one who searches for enlightenment becomes a hunter with a net who sits concealed in the shrubbery waiting for his victim to come unexpectedly down the path. Here the victim is our own unknown mind and the net is our empirical, observable self that will hang its trophy on the wall of our attainments. This will be the greatest catch yet—our own mind!

The act of meditation as here presented can also be likened to the act of sitting alone before a closed door that stands at the very center of one's own head, in the very place that separates the observable, available mind from the secret, unconscious, unavailable, inner mind. One sits and sits. One gazes and gazes. The knob slowly begins to turn. One holds one's breath in anticipation. Suddenly the door flies open and there is the hidden guest—one's own self finally in the open to be seized and carried off to show our friends.

The third wrong attitude hits upon the false self's most fundamental error regarding the void in which enlightenment takes place. This error is again centered upon the insistence of the false self that only what is possessed is real. Merton says that one sits in meditation industriously engaged in the act of emptying the mind of all thoughts so as to reach an illusive state of emptiness. But, says Merton, the whole undertaking is actually the "clinging and possessive ego-consciousness, seeking to affirm itself in 'liberation.' "[30]

This affirmation of the ego is an attempt

> to outwit reality by rejecting the thoughts (the ego) "possesses" and emptying the mirror of the mind, which it also "possesses." Thus "the mind" will be in "emptiness" and "poverty." But in reality, *"emptiness" itself is regarded as a possession, and an "attainment."* So the ego-consciousness is able, it believes, to eat its cake and have it . . . to enjoy its own narcissism under the guise of "emptiness" and "contemplation."[31]

We see here that the word "emptiness" is a trap for the false self which, rather than affirming itself on the stock market or in breaking a world record, chooses to affirm itself in emptiness.

But the emptiness the false self imagines it is attaining is wrongly sought as an attainment, and by that very fact made into the opposite of what it actually signifies, which is a fullness beyond all possession—a void "so full it is empty."

In *Zen and the Birds of Appetite* Merton once again stresses the folly that lies at the center of this falsified notion of emptiness:

> We doubtless admit that in transcending itself the ego does indeed go "beyond" itself, but in the end this proof of spiritual elasticity is all to its own credit. The further it can go without snapping, the better and more respectable ego it is. In fact, the ego trains itself to be so completely elastic that it can stretch itself almost to the vanishing point and still come back and chalk up another experience on the score card. In this case, however, there is no real self-transcendence. The "trip" that is taken is ultimately a release for and an intensification of ego-consciousness.[32]

It is in God that we rediscover and regain all we have surrendered in order to be united to him. And it is in prayer that we discover ourselves in God. Prayer is a journey in which—if God wills that we take only one step—one step places us in Paradise. Likewise, if God wills we take only one step, but we take two, we find ourselves in the depths of hell—the hell of the false self that prays not to find God but only to find and establish yet one more way of finding itself.

The enthusiastic search for experiences and attainments has little or nothing to do with true prayer. Such attempts almost always represent the "Holy Object" that "must be destroyed in so far as it is an idol embodying the secret desires, aspirations and powers of the ego-self."[33]

Mystical union is a reality. It is a grace. It is part of the holiness of the Church, but the self that attains it is not the ego but "a void in which the light of God . . . His Being and Love are manifested."[34] Mystical union is a treasure, but only if God is our treasure because we are God's treasure. The treasure is love freely given. It is found by going out of ourselves, not in order to return and chalk up another experience on a score card, but by realizing that the score card itself is a golden calf worshipped by someone who does not even exist.

Thus, Merton holds that there is an entrance into the awareness of God. But the question he raises is: *Who* is it that enters it? He tells us that it is not the self that stands anything to gain by such an achievement. It is not the self we imagine ourselves to be. It is rather the true self, the self whose identity lies hidden in God and whose identity is revealed only in union with God. And in this revelation there is no observer, but only communion and consummation in love.

4.The Realization of the True Self

God's enduring presence places the false self in a blessed insecurity. The false self is like a drop of stagnant water thrown into the raging furnace of the love of God. Even in our sins, in God's eyes we remain the great pearl for which he has lost all upon the cross in order to possess us as his own. Even in the midst of revolt, we remain his one lost sheep for which he has wandered in the wastes of death in order to bring us back to his fold.

God never does violence to the essential freedom by which we can negate ourselves as persons made in his image. But the nature of his love is such that his affirmation of us always overwhelms our negation of him. His loving advance, his covenant love (*hesed*) envelops and upholds us more assuredly than our next breath.

In this is our hope that nothing shall "separate us from the love of God which comes to us in Christ Jesus, our Lord" (Rom 8:39). In this is our joy that regardless of how distorted our hearts have become, regardless of what our conscience holds against us "God is greater than hearts" (1 Jn 3:20). After one glance of his love, our false self, in spite of all its apparent imbeddedness, dissolves away like a bad dream. That's all it is anyway—a bad dream that passes with the dawning of God's love. Our weakness remains, but it is a handed-over weakness, made strong in its openness and abandonment to God's mercy.

This simultaneous presence of light and darkness, of truth and falsity is one of the paradoxes of spiritual life. Referring first to the true self, Merton says,

> Since our inmost "I" is the perfect image of God, then when that "I" awakens, he finds within himself the Presence of Him Whose image he is. And, by a paradox beyond all human expression, God and the soul seem to have but one single "I." They are (by divine grace) as though one single person. They breathe and live and act as one. "Neither" of the "two" is seen as object.[1]

But then he adds the experiential context in which the awareness of this true self takes place and the solution of the apparent dilemma this experience entails,

> To anyone who has full awareness of our "exile" from God, our alienation from this inmost self, and our blind wandering in the "region of unlikeness," this claim can hardly seem believable. Yet, it is nothing else but the message of Christ calling us to awake from sleep, to return from exile, and find our true selves within ourselves, in that inner sanctuary which is his temple and his heaven, and (at the end of the prodigal's homecoming journey) the "Father's house."[2]

And so we must come to recognize and acknowledge our false self, but even more to acknowledge the true self that sleeps within us like Lazarus in the tomb waiting for the voice of Jesus to awaken us to life.

No one knows what first stirs in the tombs of those

awakened by God's incessant call. The first moment of
conversion (*metanoia*) is the hidden gift that can, as with
Paul, knock us to the ground, or as with Augustine, move
us to tears by the song of children and a word of scripture.
Or, as is often the case, this call of God is like a gradual,
subtle, stirring that grows within us, perhaps unnoticed,
like a small flower unfolding in an enclosed garden.

God plants this seed. It is he that makes it grow, but
he does so only with our cooperation. We must help to
bring about this awakening within us.

II

How can we give birth to the true self? How can we
emerge from our falsity and assume our true identity devoid
of all illusory self-seeking? The question reveals the supreme practicality of the spiritual life, the practicality of
the drowning man who does not hesitate to drop his treasure
in order to grasp a rope. The Buddha's well-known fire
sermon speaks of the whole world and everything in it as
being on fire. The question, he says, is whether or not we
can get out while there is still time. The great question of
life is: Can we choose life instead of death and then bring
our choice to an effective conclusion? Here methods, techniques, ideas and spiritualities of themselves are of little
use. We must not stand in the burning house with a dic-
tionary thinking we are safe because we are frantically
looking up the definition for a fire extinguisher!

Merton once told me that so few of us are willing to
become people of prayer because so few of us are willing
to go beyond definitions and concepts to grasp life itself.
There comes a time when one must set out in earnest to
return to the Father's house, to find his way out of the
burning building, to choose life instead of death.

But once we ask ourselves how to make an effective

existential choice for life instead of death we are faced with the equally disturbing question of *who* it is that is asking. In other words, the danger is always that the questions proceed from the false self and hence they do not represent a desire for deliverance at all, but only a thinly veiled attempt of the ego to stake out new and broader spiritual boundaries of its domain.

In the following text, Merton is speaking about Zen, but the point he is making pertains directly to what we are discussing here:

> Where there is carrion lying, meat-eating birds circle and descend. Life and death are two. The living attack the dead, to their own profit. The dead lose nothing by it. They gain too, by being disposed of. Or they seem to, if you must think in terms of gain and loss. Do you then approach the study of Zen with the idea that there is something to be gained by it? . . . Where there is a lot of fuss about "spirituality," "enlightenment" or just "turning on," it is often because there are buzzards hovering around a corpse. This hovering, this circling, this descending, this celebration of victory is not what is meant by the study of Zen—even though they may be a highly useful exercise in other contexts. And they enrich the birds of appetite.
>
> Zen enriches no one. There is no body to be found. The birds may come and circle for a while in the place where it is thought to be. But they soon go elsewhere. When they are gone, the "nothing," the "no-body" that was there, suddenly appears. That is Zen. It was there all the time but the scavengers missed it, because it was not their kind of prey.[3]

The birds of appetite soar about aimlessly within us.

They are flesh-eating birds and they quickly descend upon any achievement that they think will satiate their endless hunger. The desire for realization of the true self draws their attention and they gather, circling about our hope for deliverance, waiting to consume this true self, this liberation, which they hope will be exposed to their view. But Merton tells us this true self is "no-body" and the birds of appetite soon fly elsewhere. It is only then the true self appears.

Merton stresses this same point elsewhere, saying of the false self that,

> If such an "I" one day hears about "contemplation" he will perhaps set himself to "become a contemplative." That is, he will wish to admire, in himself, something called contemplation. And in order to see it, he will reflect on his alienated self. He will make contemplative faces at himself like a child in front of a mirror. . . . Sad is the case of that exterior self that imagines himself contemplative. . . . He will assume varied attitudes, and meditate on the inner significance of his own postures, and try to fabricate for himself a contemplative identity: and all the while there is nobody there. There is only an illusory, fictional "I" which seeks itself, struggles to create itself out of nothing, maintained in being by its own compulsion and the prisoner of his private illusion.[4]

Thus it is understandable that Merton could say: "Perhaps the best way to become a contemplative would be to desire with all one's heart to be anything but a contemplative; who knows?"[5]

The spiritual life must be approached with our right hand not knowing what our left hand is doing. The mystic knows little or nothing about mysticism in the sense of concerning himself with experiences and techniques. Rather the mystic is simply one who sees things as they are; he sees all of life as coming from God, sustained by God, and returning back to God. Only with this detachment from our own progress, and only in freedom from all techniques that feed the birds of appetite, can we hope to find our true self in God. Merton writes,

> The inner self is precisely that self which cannot be tricked or manipulated by anyone, even the devil. He (the true self) is like a very shy wild animal that never appears at all whenever an alien presence is at hand, and comes out only when all is peaceful, in silence, when he is untroubled and alone. He cannot be lured by anyone or anything, because he responds to no lure except that of the divine freedom.[6]

This beautiful image of the true self as a "shy wild animal" echoes the image from the Song of Songs of which Saint John of the Cross was so fond: "My lover is like a gazelle or a young stag. Here he stands behind our wall, gazing through the windows, peering through the lattices" (Sg 2:9).

The shy and illusive gazelle is not frightened by his own image on the surface of the lake, nor is he made skittish by the wind that sways the trees. But one distant footfall of the false self sends him into unreachable obscurity. One breath of self seeking, one trace of the false self's acrid wiles and the true self becomes the nobody that is not there.

III

But what is it that draws our shy and elusive inner self to the lattice, if not love? "God is love" and the true self is a self "in love." God loves us with an everlasting love

and it is his love that first creates us. It is his love that
leads him to seek us out, to consummate the wedding in
which we become who we are. But how are we to avoid
chasing him away? The false self's self-styled grimace, the
false self's plans of deceit, all the false self can do or say
closes up the lattice, blocking our view of the beloved and
keeping him far from us. How can we avoid these tactics
that keep our realization of the true self far from us?

The false self would have the answer lie in some
esoteric secret, some strenuous and bizarre technique that
would force the inner self into the open. But Merton assures
us that the opposite is true. He would have us realize that
the birth of the true self is as secret as the birth of a fawn.
It takes place in hiding. The secret birth is God's action
and therefore no action of our own can force God into
revealing himself to us. Nor can we force God to reveal
his most secret treasure, which is our own true self.

Merton tells us that in seeking realization of our true
self in prayer

> We should not look for a "method" or "sys-
> tem," but cultivate an "attitude," an "outlook":
> *faith,* openness, attention, reverence, expectation,
> supplication, trust, joy. All these finally permeate
> our being with love in so far as our *living faith*
> tells us we are in the presence of God, that we live
> in Christ, that in the Spirit of God we "see" God
> our Father without "seeing." We know him in
> "unknowing." *Faith* is the bond that unites us
> to him in the Spirit who gives us light and love.
> (Italics added.)[7]

The emphasis here is on *faith.* Faith itself is a gift of
the Spirit given to us in Christ. And it is faith that first
allows us to begin our spiritual life which is "nothing else
but Christ living in us, by his Holy Spirit."[8] The birth of

this inner realization is one with the birth of faith in us. In faith we find a certain, yet dark inner realization of that relationship that holds the secret of our ultimate identity. In faith the weight is shifted from our own poor ego into the infinite abyss of God, in whom alone we find our ultimate self, and our consummate joy. In faith we find ourselves in darkness, but a darkness in which God clasps our hand. We hear his silent breathing, one with our own, and in dark luminosity feel his eyes penetrating to the depths of our soul.

Of faith and its importance in our life, Merton writes:

> Even if everything else goes . . . provided you have your Faith, and are united with others in Faith in a Christian community of some sort, you have everything. Nothing can take it away. Nothing can take away what you are. You have to develop it yourself with God's grace. What you have to work at is your prayer. . . . What you have to do is simple. It centers around Faith. Develop your Faith.[9]

Our false self dwells in a darkness which it proclaims to be the one true light—". . . and the Light shines in the darkness and the darkness grasps it not." Thus in faith our false self is bewildered, confused and lost in a light it can neither endure nor comprehend. This light, however, is intuitively recognized by our true self to be the true light that restores our vision, heals us and returns us to the Father.

It is the soft light just before dawn in which our shy and elusive inner self gazes through the lattice, communicating to us the first silent syllables of the unspeakable secret that "the eye wherein I see God is the same eye wherein God sees me."[10]

Of this faith Merton writes,

> The more perfect faith is, the darker it be-
> comes. . . . Our certainty increases with this
> obscurity, yet not without anguish and even ma-
> terial doubt, because we do not find it easy to
> subsist in a void in which our natural powers
> have nothing of their own to rely on. And it is
> in the deepest darkness that we most fully possess
> God on earth, because it is then that our minds
> are most truly liberated. . . . it is then that we
> are filled with His infinite Light which is pure
> darkness to our reason.

> In this greatest perfection of faith the infi-
> nite God Himself becomes the Light of the dark-
> ened soul and possesses it entirely with His Truth.
> And at this inexplicable moment the deepest
> night becomes day and faith turns into under-
> standing.[11]

Merton once remarked that at night our vision is re-
versed from what it is during the day. During the day the
things that are close to us are clear and visible. But at
night, while we stumble about over things that are near us,
the stars (invisible during the day) shine in the heavens
with a clear and delicate clarity. Faith is like this. In the
dark night of faith we find our ego-self stumbling about
over itself, lost to all that was reassuring and familiar. And
yet the ultimate self, the self we are destined to become,
the true self in God, finds a clarity that is discovered this
side of death only by faith. In faith we are given an obscure
vision of the secret of our own deepest self made one with
God through Christ.

The deep and obscure promise of faith is the source
of *hope* which itself is also a gift of God and another important attitude or stance in the spiritual life. Hope is the
death of despair and the basis for hope is found in faith.
The promise of God offers us not a treasure found "out

there" beyond death, as though life were a linear path lined with thorns that ends in some unknown prize. Rather, our faith calls upon us to die even now, so that, as we die, we realize that the fruition of our hope in faith is the fruition that even now unfolds within us. God holds in his one eternal moment both our life and our death. There is only the moment, and it is God's moment. Even now we hover over the bottomless abyss of God's love. Even now by faith we lose our footing and fall into a new, unending center in which we are upheld by God and not by the narrow base of our ego's self-assertion.

No longer drawing our identity and life from what lies behind us but stretching forward toward our goal, we find that faith and hope meet each other, embrace, and sustain us. They become the feet with which we walk across the void and with abandon fall into it, lost to all but God.

This falling into God through faith is our retracing of Adam's journey, in which he fell out of faith by refusing to believe in God. Adam passed through the center of himself, placing himself between himself and God. He thus gained someone to grasp, to see, to control—someone he imagined himself to be. In reality this was but a shadow behind which he hid from God. Our faith is God's gift. When it is accepted and lived, it dissolves the shadow of the false self.

Faith and hope are themselves fulfilled only in love. As Saint Paul expresses it, "There are in the end three things that last: faith, hope and love, and the greatest of these is love" (1 Cor 13:13). This love, which is the ultimate consummation of the true self, is first of all God himself, who is love. When God gives us the Spirit, we receive the power to love God with God's own love. We are given a new identity, because this love given to us by God is in the end our very self created in the image of love. Contemplation is nothing less than that surrender, that abandon, that letting go of self to love in order to realize a deeper self born of love. "Who Am I?" asked Merton, and he responds, "I am one loved by Christ."[12] It is Christ's love for us that establishes the true self's reality. Forever the son beholds the Father in the unity of the Holy Spirit. In giving us his love, Christ gives us this Spirit and we find ourselves even now participating in God's own divine life through love.

Merton is cautious here not to violate the revealed mystery of creation. He is not proposing a vague form of pantheism. He holds that our created nature remains distinct from God. As he expresses it in speaking of mystical union,

> Even when the soul is mystically united with God there remains, according to Christian theology, a distinction between the nature of the soul and the nature of God. Their perfect unity is not then a fusion of natures, but a unity of love and of experience.[13]

While maintaining a careful distinction of natures, Merton holds for a perfect unity of love that amounts to mystical identification with God. Love makes us one spirit with God. God is love and it is in love alone that we will find the full significance of what it means to be a person, that is, to be like God.

The love we speak of not only unites us with God but to our brothers and sisters as well. Indeed, the incarnation of Jesus teaches us that we must search for God's love in human flesh and weakness. The nearest "thou" at hand is an epiphany, a manifestation of God's love. The Samaritan going from Jerusalem to Jericho found a man half dead who had been beaten by robbers. As the Samaritan bound up his wounds, Christ met Christ. Weakness met strength and both found hope in life beyond division and fear. As Merton expresses it, "Love is the epiphany of God in our poverty."[14]

By our love and our need for love we become for one another midwives of the true self. In our response to the outstretched hand we touch the infinite. And this is why it is possible to say that our real gurus, our real spiritual directors, are those people in our life who place upon us unexplainable burdens. And we find a guru in ourselves as well when we see ourselves in our poverty, in need of the friendship, the support, or the simple presence of others.

In the eyes of the one we love and in the eyes of the one who loves us we see reflected a glimmer of the true self. In genuine love for others, we go out of ourselves and find a new center in the center of the loved one who stands before us as an epiphany of God. This love manifests our true self for it does not spring from the ego but from God. It is a "disinterested" love. Of this love Merton writes,

> There is in the human will an innate tendency, an inborn capacity for disinterested love. This power to love another for his own sake is one of the things that make us like God, because this power is the one thing in us that is free from all determination. It is a power which transcends and escapes the inevitability of self-love.[15]

This love, though deeply rooted in our very identity as persons, is unavailable to us. It is like a treasure buried deep in the recesses of our own heart where we are unable to go. The gift of the Spirit of love makes access to this love possible. In the Unity of the Holy Spirit the three persons of the Trinity are one. By sharing the Spirit we too are one with God in Christ. And it is in the Incarnation of Christ that our love for God is made one with our love for others. Though love for God in contemplation calls for an essential interiority and inner silence, this inner silence and communion with God are not opposed to our love for others but become its very source.

The stirring of leaves in the wind makes the wind visible. Their stirring is the wind's stirring, their whisper is the wind's whisper. And so with love. Our actions of love make the invisible visible. Our actions of love make love present to ourselves and to others. And as we go out of ourselves in love, and become, as it were, lost in those we love, we discover a self greater than our isolated ego. We discover the birth of that self born of the death to self-centeredness.

This love proceeds from and is grounded in the love of Christ, who, in prayer, reveals to us that his love forms our deepest identity. It is this love proceeding from Christ who is "our own deepest and most intimate 'self' "[16] that forms the foundation both of interior prayer and of our love for others. Both true prayer and love for others are selfless, in that they lead us toward and emerge from a simultaneous death to self and discovery of a new self born of God. Both prayer and service to others reveal to us the tremendous truth that to be a person is to be a gift, and to give that gift is to receive the gift of being a person.

IV

An unborn baby that could think and have its way might choose not to be born. The violent wrenching from its dark, warm world into a horizon beyond its fingertips might seem like a transformation too great to bear. Yet, mercifully, there is no choice given. The child finds itself, screaming in protest, flung by the heels into an unfamiliar world.

The spiritual life is a kind of birth. In fact, Jesus proclaimed that unless we are born again we will never enter into that life that knows no death. But every birth is a kind of dying. Every new stage of growth calls for a letting go of what went before it. And this letting go hurts. The cross is the source of life yet it pierces us and drains us of the only life we know.

The Father, Jesus said, prunes every fruit tree clean to increase its yield. Prayer unveils our heart, allowing it to be cut by God's delicate touch. There is no growth in prayer without some degree of exposure to this purification process out of which the true self emerges in its unexpected splendor.

The journey into prayer is a journey directed toward a fundamental ". . . return to the heart, finding one's deepest center, awakening the profound depths of our being in the presence of God who is the source of our being and our life."[17]

In prayer we sit alone and empty. As we sit, though nothing happens, there is a subtle parting of a curtain. As lightly as a falling blossom lands upon the water, we touch down upon the kingdom of the heart. We enter into the domain of the spirit that stands within, yet beyond all that is observable and logical. We sit in a solitary exposure to the force of time not softened by distractions, to the enveloping silence not broken by chatter. Above all, we sit with a growing, unfolding desire, a waiting that is vast. Even the one who waits with patient urgency does not know or even try to know what it is that must appear.

Desire, prompted by God's grace, brings us to the emptiness that proves to be the nuptial chamber of silent prayer. As Merton expresses it,

> All the paradoxes about the contemplative
> way are reduced to this one: being without desire

means being led by a desire so great that it is in-
comprehensible. It is too huge to be completely
felt. It is a blind desire, which seems like a desire
for "nothing" only because nothing can content
it. And because it is able to rest in no-thing, then
it rests, relatively speaking, in emptiness.[18]

A contemplative spirit is not content with anything
that can be felt or comprehended: the peripheral, the passing, the half-true, all that will end instead of being fulfilled
by death. All of this, as it were, pales and dies in the face
of the one desire that shimmers in the emptiness. This
prayer calls us to walk dry-shod with the Israelites across
the bottom of the sea. Like "a man in the divided sea" we
walk on, leaving far behind us the shore of certitude. While
on both sides stand walls of water that could at any moment
sweep over us, leaving us buried in the unknown depths of
our own inscrutable mystery. It is here we learn what
faith means. It is here we discover that by faith we can
stand alone and lost, yet know all the while that the Father
holds us and will never let us go. An essential aspect of
our purification in prayer is the quiet acceptance of this
enigmatic emptiness that foils all our plans and leaves us
at a loss to know for certain whether or not we even have
a spiritual life to worry about. We find we are called upon
to lose all, even God, even ourselves as a kind of imaginary
vessel that is going to one day possess God. We discover
in the purifying stillness of prayer what Merton means when
he tells us,

> We cannot arrive at the perfect possession
> of God in this life, and that is why we are travel-
> ling and in darkness. But we already possess Him
> by grace, and therefore in that sense we have
> arrived and are dwelling in the light.
> But oh! How far have I to go to find You in
> Whom I have already arrived!

> For now, oh my God, it is to You alone that
> I can talk, because nobody else will understand.
> I cannot bring any other man on this earth into
> the cloud where I dwell in Your light, that is,
> Your darkness, where I am lost and abashed. I
> cannot explain to any other man the anguish
> which is Your joy nor the loss which is the Pos-
> session of You, nor the distance from all things
> which is the arrival in You, nor the death which
> is the birth in You because I do not know any-
> thing about it myself and all I know is that I
> wish it were over—I wish it were begun.
>
> You have contradicted everything. You
> have left me in no-man's land.[19]

Our ever-repeated turning toward Christ becomes like the waves of the ocean that pound against the jagged rocks, making them smooth. Our fidelity to the stillness of prayer washes away the concealing silt of the false self, exposing before our eyes the obscure promise of that unexpected moment in which we find in ourselves not just ourselves but him.[20]

The false self fears such a total transformation: "the external self fears and recoils from what is beyond it and above it. It dreads the alluring emptiness and darkness of the interior self."[21]

Here I stand alone. God's hand rests upon me, upon my very heart, upon the linchpin that holds "my" and "self" together. In this silent stillness at the center of the world I come to realize that life and death are at stake. I realize that it is not sufficient simply to alter or hand over this or that aspect of my life to God. He asks of me my heart. He asks of me to change my heart so that I might discover my darkness to be transformed by and made one with his light.

This change of heart is an in-depth *metanoia* that results in what the monastic fathers referred to as *purity of heart.* In the following passage Merton not only describes purity of heart, but he also equates this purity with a new identity—the true self. He says purity of heart is

> an unconditional and totally humble surrender to God, a total acceptance of ourselves and of our situation as willed by him. It means the renunciation of all deluded images of ourselves, all exaggerated estimates of our own capacities, in order to obey God's will. . . . *Purity of heart* is then correlative to a new spiritual identity—the "self" as recognized in the context of realities willed by God—Purity of heart is the enlightened awareness of the new man as opposed to the complex and perhaps rather disreputable fantasies of the old man.[22]

As we struggle more and more to expose our hearts to God's purifying action within us we discover for ourselves that even now, in mystery, what is last is first, what is least is greatest, what is cast off as useless is our only treasure. And this is so because of our own most secret identity which is given to us by God. As Merton expresses it,

> To say I am made in the image of God is to say that love is the reason for my existence, for God is love.
>
> Love is my true identity. Selflessness is my true self. Love is my true character. Love is my name.[23]

But this revelation which is obscurely given to us in the silence of solitary prayer is accompanied by a corresponding revelation of our own alienation from this love that forms our very identity. We discover in the light of God's love a dark night, a chasm, a wilderness into which God calls us in order to purify us of the opaque resistance and unreality of the false self. By *compunction* and *dread* we come to recognize within ourselves:

> confused, metaphysical awareness of a *basic antagonism between the self and God* due to estrangement from him by perverse attachment to a "self" which is mysterious and illusory.[24]

All of this may seem very dark, indeed. And, in fact, Merton has no reservations in expressing just how dark it can become as we expose ourselves to God's purifying action within us:

> The only full and authentic purification is that which turns a man completely inside out, so that he no longer has a self to defend, no longer an intimate heritage to protect against inroads and dilapidations . . . the full maturity of the spiritual life cannot be reached unless we first pass through the dread, anguish, trouble, and fear that necessarily accompany the inner crisis of "spiritual death" in which we finally abandon our attachment to our exterior self and surrender completely to Christ.[25]

Merton speaks of those God calls to contemplative prayer by saying:

> God brings these people into the way of life by depriving them of the light and the consolation which they seek, by impeding their own efforts, by confusing and depriving them of the satisfactions which their own efforts aim to attain. Thus blocked and frustrated, unable to carry on with their accustomed projects, they find themselves in a very painful state in which their own wishes, their self-esteem, their presumption, their aggressivity and so on are systematically humiliated.

What is worse, they cannot understand how this comes about! They do not know what is happening to them. It is here that they must decide whether to go on in the way of prayer under the secret guidance of grace, in the night of pure faith, or whether they will go back to a form of existence in which they can enjoy familiar routines and retain an illusory sense of their perfect autonomy in perfectly familiar realms, without having to remain subject to the obedience of faith in these trying and baffling circumstances proper to the "dark night."[26]

Genuine prayer calls upon us to respond to our lot with greater faith, waiting with great expectancy for God's deliverance. But all bogus mysticism knows nothing of such waiting. It wants nothing to do with the whole purifying process being discussed here. When confronted with this emptiness the false self responds by reaching out for the forbidden fruit. This gesture is exemplified by the

pseudo-mystic who flees into his own inner darkness and tries to wall himself up inside his own silence. There he seeks to enjoy the false sweetness of a narcissistic seclusion, and does indeed enjoy it for a while, until he learns too late that he has poisoned himself with the fruit of the tree that is forbidden. . . . This indeed is the forbidden tree: this tree of self which grows in the middle of Paradise but which we ourselves are not supposed to see or notice. All the other trees are there . . . of them we can be aware. . . . But if we become aware of ourselves, turn back too much upon ourselves, and seek to rest in ourselves, then we take the fruit that was forbidden us: we become "as gods knowing good and evil," for we find division within ourselves and are cut off from external reality at the same time.[27]

But the dark night does more than simply move us to become detached from all narcissistic self-seeking. All this talk of purification is not simply a matter of realizing that "The contemplative life is a life of intense inner conflict. The peace which it brings is a peace that follows war, and it exists often enough in the midst of war."[28]

Nor is this dark night but an esoteric terror beyond all endurance. The God who purifies us purifies us with love. The purification is a subtle affair which is at times almost imperceptible. Though hours of intense darkness do indeed exist, there remains a general tone that is wholly undramatic. Life goes on. There remains a fundamental level of happiness that remains untouched, is even at times deepened by the purifying emptiness of prayer. The cleansing action of God is a gentle one carried out by a gentle God who desires only our happiness through our union with himself.

The night not only purifies us from our attachments to our own spiritual plans; it not only reveals to us that yoke that is light and easy to carry. It also proves to be the prelude to perfect joy. We discover in time and through God's grace that it is the darkness surrounding us which is in fact the light of God. It is our awareness of our sinfulness that reveals to us just how good the Good News really is. We discover that, without realizing it, the dark night emptied us of our own petty concerns, even of our own petty self, to allow us to be filled with desire for the one thing necessary. Out of darkness emerges our true self, the self that cherishes this one thing and finds unceasing delight in it.

In solitary prayer we meet our self head on in a dark, inner battle. It is as though Michael and Lucifer live within and wage their conflict upon the fields of our heart. A deep insight into the true nature of this battle is found in Merton's reflection upon the text of Genesis depicting Jacob's battle with God. Merton refers to this battle as

the "prototype of all spiritual battles."[29] The text on which
Merton comments reads,

> He (Jacob) remained alone: and behold a
> man wrestled with him till morning. And when
> he saw that he could not overcome him, he
> touched the sinew of his thigh and forthwith it
> shrank. And he said to him: Let me go, for it
> is break of day. He answered: I will not let go
> except thou bless me. And he said: What is thy
> name? He answered: Jacob. But he said: Thy
> name shall not be called Jacob but Israel: for
> thou hast been strong against God. How much
> more shalt thou prevail against men? Jacob asked
> him: Tell me by what name are thou called? He
> answered: Why dost thou ask me my name? And
> he blessed him in the same place (Gen 32:24-
> 29).[30]

Jacob is alone, as if in solitude in the dark night, and
suddenly without warning he is engaged in conflict. His
adversary is mysterious—called both a man and God. His
adversary wounds him, yet blesses him. Moreover, he gives
him a new identity.

Merton beautifully applies the biblical prototype to
the dark night of prayer and describes his insight in terms
of the true and false self:

> The battle is with "man" and yet it is with
> God, for it is the battle of our exterior self with
> the interior self, the "agent" which is the likeness
> of God in our soul and which appears at first
> sight to be utterly opposed to the only self we
> know. It is the battle of our own strength lodged
> in the exterior self, with the strength of God
> which is the life and actuality of our interior self.
> And in the battle, which takes place in the dark-
> ness of night, the angel, the inner self, wounds

a nerve in our thigh so that afterward we limp. Our natural powers are restricted and crippled. We are humbled and made ignorant. We see that we have become foolish and that even in good works we limp and are feeble. But also, though we are drawn to evil, we no longer have the power to run swiftly in pursuit of it. Yet we have power over our antagonist to the extent that though we cannot overcome him, yet we do not let him go until he blesses us. This power is more than our own strength, it is the power of love, and it secretly comes from within, from the antagonist Himself. It is with his own power with which he wishes to be held by us. It is the power by which he is "reached and held close" according to the *Cloud of Unknowing*. It makes us "strong against God" and merits for us a new name, Israel, which means "He who sees God." And this new name is what makes us contemplatives—it is a new being and a new capacity for experience. Yet when we ask the name of our antagonist we cannot know it, for even our own inmost self is unknown, just as God Himself is unknown.[31]

And so the true nature of the struggle of the dark night begins to appear. The great revelation is that, if our struggle is authentic, we find we are not alone. We struggle in solitude with a self that is more than ourselves and this secret antagonist with which our external self struggles is at once ourselves and God. The struggle is in fact a blessing, a blessing that arises in a new being and a new capacity for experience.

This new being is our own true self in Christ and this new experience is the contemplation of God in Christ. Or better still, it is our ability to participate in Christ's contemplation of the Father in the unity of the Holy Spirit.

And so the dark night proves to be in fact a bridal chamber in whose darkness Christ, the antagonist with the name of both God and man, wounds us and gives us a new self. He wounds us in our sharing of his desolation and death upon the cross. And he weds us to himself so that with him and in him, his life becomes our own.

V

While in his hermitage preparing to go down to the monastery to give the monks a talk on poetry, Merton wrote, "They will listen with attention thinking some other person is talking about some other poem."[32] In a sense we can say this other person was a more or less innocent version of the false self. This other person is Merton the author, Merton the poet, Merton the man of accomplishment.

The real Merton achieved nothing, yet achieved all things. The real Merton was not this and not that. The real Merton spent his day living a "day of a stranger" and this stranger left himself his own legacy when he wrote, "What I do is live. How I pray, is breathe"[33]—a colossal achievement consciously attained by few.

Merton, the man of title, addresses a sermon to the birds, saying "Esteemed friends, birds of noble lineage, I have no message to you accept this: be what you are: be *birds*. Thus you will be your own sermon to yourselves!" But it is Merton the stranger who knew very well the full import of the birds' gentle reprimand: "Even this is one sermon too many!"[34]

We cannot reach the stars in a rowboat, nor can we drink up the entire ocean with a sieve. Much less can we say in words what can be heard only after all words have fallen into silence. And so the validity of Merton's words rests in the hope that the words will prompt the occasion in which God will grant the mysterious " 'something' that is born of silence."[35] Or, perhaps more to the point, the validity of Merton's message rests in the hope that the words will point to that self that speaks in silence and hears only in silence its own secret name.

Like all great religious figures, Merton's greatness lies in the fact that he pointed to the one thing great in all of us. His life and words form a kind of mirror in which we can behold our deepest, yet forgotten self. Surely all we have said of Merton will point to the fact that, beyond his personality, beyond his talents and achievements, we have to see a self-beyond self, in which is grounded the ultimate validity and verification of all he did and said.

Merton's whole life can be seen as a witness to his central message that,

> if you are to penetrate your own silence and dare to advance without fear into the solitude of your own heart, and risk the sharing of that solitude with the lonely other who seeks God through you and with you, then you will truly recover the light and the capacity to understand what is beyond words . . . it is the intimate union in the depths of your own heart, of God's spirit and your own secret inmost self, so that you and He are in all truth One Spirit.[36]

It is in contemplation that we penetrate our own silence, that we dare to advance without fear into the solitude of our own heart. As if we were sinking beneath the waves of a turbulent sea, we discover in turning within the Alpha and Omega, the enduring Presence that embraces all that is real. This penetration into ourselves is itself a grace and not a technique. It is fearsome and uncanny . . . yet it is the source of a peace and fulfillment beyond all expression. It is new . . . yet for the first time we find ourself at home. It is perfect stillness. . . yet it is the source of all action. It confirms all we do that is genuine . . . yet it has no need to affirm itself. It is within us as the root of our being . . .

yet it is forever beyond us, calling us into ecstasies unknown. It is without name or achievement . . . yet it alone
truly enriches us. It is poor; it is empty . . . yet it alone
makes us the royalty of the Kingdom of God.

To what can we liken this union of God's Spirit and
our own spirit in our own secret inmost self? It can be
likened to nothing. Perhaps, however, a parable can give
some intimation of it: The bell in the tower swings from
life to death, from defeat to victory, from joy to sorrow.
But in the shadow of the tower stands a lone tree. It sinks
its roots not into the ringing of the bell but into the silent
earth. Its leaves sway not to proclaim a message but simply
because the wind is blowing. The tree is silent. It has no
name. It has nothing to say. It has nothing to give except
its being there.

It is in the shade of this tree that children come to
play. Their clothing picks up the tree's subtle, sweet aroma.
They breathe the tree's air, for its element is their own. As
unknowing as the sky, their eyes shine with the tree's secret
promise.

Adults gather in the shade of this tree—not those with
what Merton called a "lumberman's" mentality, for this
tree has no use. But adults do come here. They come
when the bell's ceaseless ringing becomes an unbearable din
that turns religion into politics, growth into exploitation,
and the search for a bigger and better life into a living death.

Those who wish to sit beneath this tree cannot deny
the world, or themselves, for in doing so their wagging
heads pick up the cadences of the bell and the tree withers—
vanishes from their sight. Those who wish to sit here must
neither deny nor affirm anything but pass beyond both
denial and affirmation in pure Presence.

And so, too, those Christians who sit beneath this
tree are not those who deny there is a message to proclaim.
But they are those who realize that ultimately the Good

News is that in Christ God has taken us to himself, wedded us to himself in the simple, concrete reality of our everyday lives. Now in their simple reality, our lives are divine acts in the order of graced being. We must proclaim the Good News, but above all we must be who we are in God. We must open ourselves to Christ's work in us, so as to receive the transforming realization of our true self in God, which is an

> identity that does not annihilate our own, which is ours, and yet "received." It is a Person eternally other than ourselves who identifies Himself perfectly with ourselves. This Identity is Christ, God.[37]

Christ is God in whose veins flows our blood and in whose heart is found all our hopes and fears. Christ is God who killed death, gave us the Spirit and, one with us in the spirit, makes the life he has in the Father to be ours by grace.

Merton's message is that every Christian, in his own way as willed by God, must by way of simple faith, selfless love, and humble prayer realize that the nothingness he fears is in fact the treasure he longs for. Each must realize that God is so with us as to transcend any I-Thou relationship. In a "transubjectivity"[38] he finds himself in us, and in prayer he invites us to find ourselves in him.

Before undertaking any project, assuming any stance, fulfilling any purpose, we are called upon to abide ourselves, to do what we do, to "just live," and in simple presence to life learn to expect nothing out of anything and everything out of nothing.

Prayer adds not one iota to this simple presence. On the contrary, in the darkness of faith all superstructures dissolve. It is in the letting-go, the abandonment of silent prayer that we discover that all things are already ours if we only be who we are in Christ. Merton states:

In prayer we discover what we already have. You start where you are and you deepen what you already have, and you realize that you are already there. We already have everything, but we don't know it and we don't experience it. Everything has been given to us in Christ. All we need is to experience what we already possess.[39]

Christ lived in Merton's hermitage because in his hermitage Merton was nobody except someone loved by Christ. Not the writing of his books, but his simply being there was the hidden witness to the simple central reality that each of us must realize: "we are not entirely what we seem to be, and that what appears to be our 'self' is soon going to disappear into nothingness."[40]

When Merton told me that "one thing for sure about heaven is that there is not going to be much of you there," he was, I think, referring to the mystery that even now we are in God's kingdom. And that even now we can begin to realize it if we but die to egocentric self-seeking and seek God's will with a pure heart.

Because God is everywhere he is likewise no-where, meaning there is no "where" in which we can see him "out there." Closer to us than we are to ourselves, he is too close to see. He is the heart of our heart, the hope of our hopes, the love of our love, the ground of our being.

Where must we go to see him?—Nowhere! What can we do to have him? Nothing! All we can do, at least for a moment (an eternal moment) is to abandon all doing and be who we are in him and open ourselves to his life within us. It is then we will at once see him and ourselves, for we will at once be him and ourselves in a unity of divine love. In fidelity to silent prayer there is unveiled the possibility of infinite growth in union with God. We can be so transformed through this unveiling that we existentially realize within us that "for me to live is Christ." We realize obscurely in our *being,* that our simple, concrete acts are open to a transformation through which they are "not only Godlike, but they become *God's own acts.*"[41]

There is no where to go. There is no thing to do. God is upon and within us. In the midst of our humble duties, our poor, weak selves, our simple *being* who we are, we can say with Jacob with overwhelming gratitude: "truly this is the house of God and the gate of heaven and I knew it not."

Merton's life was not a romantic adventure with a hagiographer behind every tree taking notes each time Merton blew his nose. His solitary life was a poor life, as all solitary lives must be. He woke before dawn with a mind "not totally reconciled to being out of bed."[42] He ate, worked, walked in the woods and prayed. In the winter he was cold and in the summer he was hot. And that is the true self. It is the self that is nobody, that is ordinary and poor. It is this ordinary self that is extraordinary for it is this ordinary self one with the moment, one with the concrete reality of everyday life, that is the self God creates, the poor self made rich in the poverty of the cross.

Merton's message is that each of us lives in the hermitage of our daily self. Beneath all our achievements, plans, travels, and conquests we have but life. When we drink water, when we silently watch children play, when we walk in the cold and feel cold, we are in life, one with it and hence one with God. And so no matter what we have it is always enough, for nothing is enough. No matter where we are we are no-where. No matter who we become we are nobody. For in the ground of our being we live Christ's life. In the foundations of the heart, God is present in our simple presence to life.

The great risk of all spirituality is that it so easily becomes a surrogate for being present to life. All too often the search for religious experiences and the promotion of spiritualities have become exercises in the care and feeding of sacred cows. Sacred cows are important; they are the symbolic, mythic structures that give us our social identity. They must not be abused or neglected, for they will turn on us with a vengeance of inner and social barbarism and destruction. But there is the door of prayer. There is the gate of disinterested love, the gate of Presence. It is a narrow gate. It stands at the very center of ourselves. And when we enter this land of "silent music" and "sounding solitudes" the sacred cows must rest content to graze outside the gates. By entering this land we learn to divest ourself of the sacred cows' claim on us. We learn to tend them, instead of letting them tend us. In this land we discover that it is in a total surrender of our whole life to God that we attain to the freedom of the children of God. It is in this land we discover that "We are nothing. We are everything."[43] All this is so because God is All in all and he has taken us to himself and lives in us and delights in us. We no more need a soapbox to stand on than does the moon or a single blade of grass wet with dew.

But this insight is valid only in light of the paradox of the cross. Only in death to self is there life without death. Only in great desire, in earnest prayer and in selfless love can this freedom of which we speak be found. The old man dies hard. Our heart eludes us and its darkness resents our intrusion. Faith is a death to understanding. Hope is a death to all past achievements from which we gain our identity. And charity is death to self-love. Like Jacob, we must wrestle through the night if the dawn is to bring us a blessing and a new name.

Our struggle does not remove us from our simple, everyday self but confirms its ultimate dimensions. Our prayer does not carry us off into realms unknown but reveals the unknown depths of each passing hour. Nevertheless the struggle is a real one. The realization of the true self does not fall into our lap like ripe fruit. It is true that in God we live without effort, but it is also true that it calls for a divestiture of self to live without effort. The following text not only refers to the present reality of God's presence but also to the only way for us to realize it,

> The desert becomes a paradise when it is accepted as desert. The desert can never be anything but a desert if we are trying to escape it. But once we fully accept it in union with the passion of Christ, it becomes a paradise. . . . This breakthrough into what you already have is only accomplished through the complete acceptance of the cross.[44]

Anyone who has given any degree of serious effort to silent prayer knows by experience just how desolate the desert of our heart can become. Just to endure an hour without running away, just to omit doing something practical, just to be silent, can involve a more strenuous effort than any external task.

Two errors must be avoided. On the one hand we must avoid quietism, that form of inertia in which we sit on our hands waiting for God to zap us with some unforeseeable experience. And on the other hand we must avoid a kind of spiritual activism in which we close our eyes, bite the bullet and painfully surge on to reach a goal we ourselves have determined we must reach so as to have something we do not already have.

Again the way to avoid either error is a simple purity of heart in which we go to prayer seeking not prayer but God. We go trusting in an inner wisdom that guides us in the way of desire beyond desires, of vision without illusion. Merton once told me to quit trying so hard in prayer. He said, "How does an apple ripen? It just sits in the sun."

A small green apple cannot ripen in one night by tightening all its muscles, squinting its eyes and tightening its jaw in order to find itself the next morning miraculously large, red, ripe and juicy beside its small green counterparts. Like the birth of a baby or the opening of a rose, the birth of the true self takes place in God's time. We must wait for God, we must be awake; we must trust in his hidden action within us.

From time to time a forest fire breaks out in the wooded hills surrounding the monastery. When this would occur the monks usually joined with neighboring farmers to put out the blaze. On one such occasion I was in a group of novices being led by Merton over the hills with brooms and shovels to put out the fire.

Suddenly, just as we were approaching the fire, we could hear the Angelus ringing in the distance. At the time the custom was for all the monks to say the Angelus by facing the church, kneeling, bowing over, and placing their knuckles on the ground. Much to my surprise, upon hearing the Angelus, Merton yelled out, "Stop, let's all say the Angelus!" And so with the flames in the near distance we all knuckled down and silently prayed. The very idea of it made me laugh. It all seemed so incongruous, praying there while the flames crackled and spread through the dry grass and leaves behind us.

But then it struck me that prayer is always incongruous. Unless we are willing to knuckle down before the flames we will never truly pray. The forest of our activities, plans and projects burns with demands, deadlines and the threat to consume us. There must be a clearing made for God. There must be a time for no-body within us to sit in the nothingness of simple awareness and humble prayer.

Merton once remarked that the Church and the world do not need people to talk about prayer, think about prayer or write about prayer nearly as much as they need people to pray. Until we go to pray there is no prayer. And when we go to pray we confront our poverty and our helplessness. We find we can offer only the widow's mite which is small yet great in God's eyes for it is all we have.

One cannot force the issue here. A forced determined effort to continue praying in the face of adversity, dryness and emptiness may be nothing but the false self attempting to prove its endurance. There must rather be but a simple desire for God and a humble detachment from experiences or the lack of experiences. Merton once told me that "in silent prayer we must simply realize that we are in water over our head." In these waters the false self quickly panics and heads for shore. But the true self, secure in its humility, finds these waters to be a womb from which, in an unexpected eternal moment, it is brought forth by him who makes all things new.

And so asking how to realize the true self is much like facing a large field covered with snow that has not yet been walked on and asking, "Where is the path?" The answer is to walk across it and there will be a path. One cannot find out first how to realize the true self and then set out to reach the clearly visualized goal. Rather, one must walk on in faith and as one goes on, the goal appears—not before, nor within, nor beyond us, but it does appear . . . and it appears to no-one. It appears no-where. It appears not in a revelation of a fact but a transformation of our hearts, in which, without knowing how, God transforms us into himself and we begin to realize obscurely yet deeply that our lives are hidden with Christ in God.

To what can we liken this discovery? It is like the experience of a man who, while out walking alone on a bitter cold and starless night, unexpectedly comes upon a large, warm-looking house. Upon approaching the house and pressing his face against the window, he sees himself sleeping comfortably before the fire! Suddenly, he realizes that he is trapped outside his own house. He realizes his life is rich, yet he stands impoverished. He is secure yet he stands on the edge of death. He is fulfilled yet he stands sterile and empty.

Frantically, he begins to pound upon the window, yelling loudly to be let in. But the self inside does not hear and, as he pounds, the glass barrier dividing him from his life only grows thicker and his clenched fists grow numb with pain.

At long last, realizing finally that all efforts of brute force achieve nothing, he sits quietly in the snow overcome by a growing single silent desire, by an unfaltering hope, that he might be one with himself. This desire, though appearing powerless awakens the self within and with this awakening the glass itself dissolves. The house dissolves and he discovers that he was really at home all along and did not know it. He finds the night to be in fact his light and the bitter cold to be itself a consuming fire of utter joy and fulfillment.

This discovery is the discovery of the contemplative way. It is a discovery so far beyond our understanding that it calls for the faith of a John the Baptist. John, while in prison, received word from Jesus that, "blessed are they who are not scandalized in me." In effect, John was called upon to realize that losing his head is of itself no cause for alarm. It is just his head. With faith we can lose all, even our head, and by our loss find ourselves richer than kings.

All this helps stress the wisdom in Merton's words when he writes,

> One of the greatest obstacles to your grow-
> ing is the fear of making a fool of yourself. Any
> real step forward implies the risk of failure. And
> the really important steps imply the risk of com-
> plete failure. Yet we must make them, trusting

in Christ. If I take this step, everything I have done so far might go down the drain. In a situation like that we need a shot of Buddhist mentality. Then we see, down what drain? So what? . . . . We have to have the courage to make fools of ourselves, and at the same time be awfully careful not to make fools of ourselves.[45]

We need common sense in prayer. We need to keep our feet ,on the ground, for if we lose our contact with everyday reality we greatly lessen our ability to help others and to grow in genuine union with Christ. But within this wisdom there is concealed yet another wisdom that is folly to the world both within and around us.

We must keep our feet on the ground with regard to our psychological and physical well-being. We must daily strive to better carry out our mundane duties. We must strive daily to show greater concern and love for others. But in and through all of this we must not fear falling through the center of it all: we must not be afraid to fall through the center of the world which is hidden deep within us. We must not wait for common sense, our acquaintances, or our schedules to make room for prayer and to support our efforts. If we do, prayer will never come. If we wait for the time in which to wait for God we will never wait for him. We will never discover in prayer our true self in God.

There is a paradox encountered in the contemplative's understanding of what is meant by the apparently exclusive terms of wisdom and foolishness. The contemplative is drawn to a vision in which the dichotomy between the two becomes irrelevant and meaningless: We are called to become prudent enough to embrace the folly of the cross, to become wise enough to be a fool for Christ's sake. Above all, we must see that the final resolution of the tension between wisdom and foolishness rests in our existential grasp in faith of the distinction between our external self and our true, inner self:

> The shallow "I" of individualism can be possessed, developed, cultivated, pandered to, satisfied: it is the center of all our strivings for gain and for satisfaction, whether material or spiritual. But the deep "I" of the spirit, of solitude and of love, cannot be "had," possessed, developed, perfected. It can only *be*, and *act* according to the inner laws which are not of man's contriving, but which come from God. They are the Laws of the Spirit, who, like the wind, blows where He wills. This inner "I," who is always alone, is always universal: for in this inmost "I" my own solitude meets the solitude of every other man and the solitude of God. Hence it is beyond division, beyond limitation, beyond selfish affirmation. It is only this inmost and solitary "I" that truly loves with the love and the spirit of Christ. This "I" is Christ Himself, living in us: and we, in Him, living in the Father.[46]

5. The Insight

I

The writings of the contemplative traditions of the world's great religions contain numerous examples that illustrate the importance of the relationship between master and disciple:

The disciple comes with a question, a life-and-death question which for years, weeks or moments (it does not matter) has come up against a stone wall of silence. Then, suddenly, the master speaks a single word and the wall crumbles silently into dust. He waves his hand and the wall disperses like smoke. How can this be? More precisely, how is it that one person can be the means of giving another a transforming awareness of God's presence?

This question is applicable to any direct communication of authentic religious experience. We read a book, hear a sermon, run our finger lightly over the crystalled luminous designs of a frosted window and something of God appears. Through a hidden opening he enters and the One we searched for in vain suddenly holds us, sharing with us his secret presence.

How is it that one person hears a thousand words and is bored, while another person hears but one word and finds eternal life? How is it that anyone is able to find entrance into the palace of nowhere? What is the mysterious event that takes place whenever anyone finds—in any experience, in any book or any person—a genuine encounter with God?

Merton approaches such questions by distinguishing between communication and communion as two fundamentally different modes of knowing. Communication is logical, quantitative and practical in its application. It is a linear form of human intercourse in which each piece of information is given one at a time and leads up to some particular conclusion. Mathematics is the language *par excellence* of communication. And computers are the champions of mathematical language. Computers are able to communicate vast quantities of usable, verifiable data that is unaffected by subjective thought and feeling.

We could not live without this one-dimensional mode of knowing. But, of itself, it lacks the power to convey the deepest hopes and yearnings of human existence. A wife tells her husband "I love you" not to communicate a previously unknown, logical, verifiable piece of information, but rather to articulate what it is that binds her to her spouse. The repetition of such words is not redundant. Rather, like each new rising of the sun, each new "I love you" offers new, yet-to-be-explored possibilities. Each "I love you" carries within it the promise of renewed and deepened levels of intimacy and union.

The "I love you" finds its power in its ability to express the wife's *communion* with her husband. The words themselves evoke occasions of this communion, which is a mode of knowing not wholly available to what can be communicated in quantitative, verifiable terms. Words are to communion what the sky is to the stars. The sky does not own the stars, nor contain them like coins held securely in a pouch. Rather the sky is the matrix in which the stars appear. So too, the logical content in the words "I love you" cannot account for what the words convey. They are rather the occasion for the love they express to appear.

The failure to communicate is frustration. The failure to commune is despair. Of communion Merton says, "It is something that the deepest ground of our being cries out for, and it is something for which a lifetime of striving would not be enough."[1]

In the book of Acts we read of the eunuch riding along in his carriage reading the book of Isaiah. He is approached by Philip, who asks him if he understands what he is reading. The eunuch responds by saying, "How can I, unless some man shows me?" Philip climbs into the carriage, speaks to him, and the eunuch finds not information but communion with God. He responds not by taking notes but by going down into the water to be baptized. Philip's words came to the eunuch not in the form of information but as symbols evoking an encounter with God.

Religious language may not be logical, but it is always symbolic. It is always a symbol, a promise of the communion the disciple longs to discover. The purpose of the symbol is not to convey information but to open unknown depths of awareness enabling the disciple to come upon "his own center, his own ontological roots in a mystery of being that transcends his individual ego."[2]

Of symbols and their role in religious awakening Merton writes,

> Traditionally, the value of the symbol is precisely in its apparent uselessness as a means of simple communication. It is ordered toward communion, not to communication. Because it is not an efficient mode of communicating information, the symbol can achieve a higher purpose of going beyond practicality and purpose, beyond cause and effect. Instead of establishing a new contact by a meeting of minds in the sharing of

news, the symbol tells nothing new: it revives our
awareness of what we already know, and deepens
our awareness. What is "new" in the symbol is
the ever new discovery of a new depth and a new
actuality in what is and always has been. . . . The
function of the symbol is to manifest a union
that *already exists but is not fully realized.* The
symbol awakens awareness or restores it. Therefore it does not aim at communication but at
communion. Communion is the awareness of
participation in an ontological or religious reality: in the mystery of being, of human love, of
redemptive mystery, of contemplative truth.[3]

The "union that already exists" is the true self concealed by sin. It is our personhood, our very existence as a
created capacity for perfect union with God. The symbol
evokes our identity in a "contemplative truth" that is known
by a participation in what is known. What then can be said
that will most directly evoke this religious awakening? The
answer is that both everything and nothing that can be said
may evoke it. Our union with God is our person, it is *who*
we are and not any *thing* we know. It is precisely our identity that emerges once we are freed by death from all the
things we thought ourselves to be. Therefore, nothing can
be said that, by the sheer, informational content of the
statement, could bring about awareness of our identity-
giving relationship with the living God.

Purely objective statements miss the mark, for God
is not an object. He is Person. Nor are we, as persons,
objects. Here *all* is Subject. There is no "object" "out
there" to "see." Here all is presence and communion. Here
everything, including our own individuality, remains itself—or, rather, for the first time becomes itself, but does so
only by opening out into the oneness that is God.

Only symbols can awaken our awareness of God. And
a symbol is any reality that comes to us emptied and filled

with God. We touch the symbol and it bursts into a theophany of presence.

But a book, a spiritual director, or a moment of silence cannot readily become symbols unless we prepare for God's coming. Unless we make ready for the manifestation of God, his coming will be like seed falling on rocky ground. It is faith that allows a symbol to come into its own. And faith must be nurtured and developed so as to prepare us for God's coming. Of this preparation Merton writes:

> the *pre-verbal* level . . . that of the unspoken and undefinable *preparation, the pre-disposition* of mind and heart. . . . This demands among other things a *freedom from automatisms and routines,* a candid liberation from external social dictates . . . which restrict understanding and inhibit experience of the new, the unexpected.[4]

As persons we are a communion with God. As human beings made one with Christ in the Spirit, we are ourselves a supreme symbol of God. Nothing can be added to the *all* that has been given to us as persons redeemed by Christ. But the *all* never violates our freedom and everything can be added by our decision to accept all that has been given us. Our whole spiritual life is this opening of ourselves to be existentially, consciously, concretely fulfilled by the communion with God that constitutes our own deepest reality.

God is our *all*. Yet so often our aggressive daily routines shatter the delicate treasure of God's presence. Our habits are cataracts that obscure our vision. Our useless labor creates calluses that prevent us from sensing the light touch of God's hand.

By daily fidelity to inner silence and solitude the Spirit frees us from these tyrannies. In silence we allow God to till the fields of our heart. In silence we discover that the next blink of our eye is the gate of heaven. In silence there is no routine, for in silence everything is all at once. Everything is new.

We read in silence; we read looking for God. But we read in a particular way. A man drops a rare diamond in the leaves of the forest floor. Carefully, he kneels down. One by one he lifts each leaf. Slowly he searches, knowing his lost treasure is in the leaves. And this is how it is that we must read, listen to another and wait in silence. Our attentive expectancy in faith brings us to the brink of the insight of our true self in God. It is this preparation that allows us to realize that all of creation is a symbol of He who is. It is this preparation as a lifelong process that fills us with God's light even as we journey on in the darkness.

Insight into the true self is not essentially a matter of astute intellectual perception. It is not a matter of thinking very hard until we have suddenly figured out a riddle. This point is brought home in the following Zen story related by Merton in *Mystics and Zen Masters.*

> A master saw a disciple who was very zealous in meditation.
>
> The master said: "Virtuous one, what is your aim in practicing *Zazen* (meditation)?"
>
> The disciple said: "My aim is to become a Buddha."
>
> Then the master picked up a tile and began to polish it on a stone in front of the hermitage.
>
> The disciple said: "What is the Master doing?"
>
> The master said: "I am polishing this tile to make it a mirror."

The disciple said: "How can you make a mirror by polishing a tile?"

The master replied: "How can you make a Buddha by practicing *Zazen?*"[5]

We can get a spiritual hernia from polishing bricks. God's fire never leaps forth from our rubbing thought against thought. In fact, the whole contemplative tradition is ordered toward bringing the aspirant to discover:

If one reaches the point where understanding fails, this is not a tragedy: it is simply a reminder to stop thinking and start looking. Perhaps there is nothing to figure out after all: perhaps we only need to wake up.[6]

Jesus bid Lazarus wake up and Lazarus, stumbling forth from his tomb, is a concrete symbol of what each of us is called to do once we hear Christ's voice. We are to stumble forth from the tomb of lethargy, blindness, doubt and duplicity into the simple light of God's call.

Prayer, as the distilled awareness of our whole life before God, is meant to lead us to a radical transformation of consciousness in which all of life becomes a symbol. All of life is seen as God sees it. All of life is seen simply as it is.

Prayer is the fertile soil in which the insight into our true self in God takes root and grows. As our true awareness grows, as we see through the eyes of the Person we are, we see with a new vision. We see the Presence of God in all that is. Each thing becomes a symbol of communion with God just by being the thing it is. Merton states this beautifully when in a moment of silence in the novitiate chapel he reflects about the

Beauty of sunlight falling on a tall vase of red and white carnations and green leaves on the altar of the novitiate chapel. The light and dark. The darkness of the fresh, crinkled flower: light, warm and red, all around the darkness. The flower is the same color as blood, but it is in no sense whatever "as red as blood." Not at all! It is as red as a carnation. Only that.

This flower, this light, this moment, this silence: *Dominus est*. Eternity. He passes. He remains. We pass. In and out. He passes. We remain. We are nothing. We are everything. He is in us. He is gone from us. He is not here. We are here in Him.

All these things can be said, but why say them?

The flower is itself. The light is itself. The silence is itself. I am myself. All, perhaps, illusion. But no matter, for illusion is the shadow of reality and reality is the grace and gift that underlies all these lights, these colors, this silence. Underlies? Is that true? They are simply real. They themselves are His gift.[7]

This text reveals a mode of awareness that needs no formulas and explanations. No ideas come between the flowers and the one who sits before them. Each thing is simply "itself." In this mode of awareness each thing is left without a name, save the secret name given to it by God. Merton writes:

Although I see the stars, I no longer pretend to know them. Although I have walked in those woods, how can I claim to love them? One by one I shall forget the names of individual things.

> You, Who sleep in my breast, are not met
> with words, but in the emergence of life within
> life and of wisdom within wisdom. You are found
> in communion: Thou in me and I in Thee and
> Thou in them and they in me: dispossession with-
> in dispossession, dispassion within dispassion,
> emptiness within emptiness, freedom within free-
> dom. I am alone. Thou art alone. The Father
> and I are One.[8]

This is insight into the true self. It is a mode of knowing, or rather a mode of existing, which is much like the
night which needs no place to hide, for it gives hiding to
all who are in it. This communion with God through simple
awareness of life as it is, is much like water which needs
not get wet because it makes all things wet that touch it.

If a man sets out on a journey to search for the tip of
his own nose his first step betrays his total blindness as to
what he seeks. So, too, Merton reminds us that God is
everywhere and is therefore never in a particular place that
is other than where we happen to be at each moment. Therefore "we do not need to leave the point where we are and
seek it (God's presence) somewhere else, but to forget all
points as equally irrelevant because to seek the unlimited in
a definite place is to limit it and hence not to find it."[9]

Once this is realized, everything becomes a potential
symbol making communion with God possible. A single
sentence read in silence, a single word, a lone bird soaring
aimlessly through a cloudless sky, a child stirring the water
with a stick—anything, anything at all can bring us to the
insight of the true self that says, "for me to live is Christ."

II

Contemplation is the true self emerging in awareness.
It is the emergence into awareness of our person, our iden-

tity-giving subsisting relationship with God. But this awareness of which we speak is not the awareness proper to the
external self. The dawn of contemplation does not bring
with it a new possession of the ego-self. Indeed, Merton
assures us that

> The true inner self, the true indestructible
> and immortal person, the true "I" who answers
> to a new and secret name known only to himself
> and to God, does not "have" anything, even "con-
> templation." This "I" is not the kind of subject
> that can amass experiences, reflect on them, re-
> flect on himself, for this "I" is not the superficial
> and *empirical* self that we know in our everyday
> life.[10]

Not only is the awareness of God in contemplation
not a possession of ego consciousness but, Merton adds,

> As long as there is an "I" that is the definite
> subject of a contemplative experience, an "I" that
> is aware of itself and its contemplation, an "I"
> that can possess a certain "degree of spirituality,"
> then we have not yet passed over the Red Sea,
> we have not yet "gone out of Egypt." We remain
> in the realm of multiplicity, activity, incomplete-
> ness, striving and desire.[11]

The awareness of contemplation is a matter of an
ontology of love. God manifests himself to himself and to
us as Trinity. And the Trinity is God's contemplation of
himself, his subsisting union with himself in the perfect
actuality of his divine existence. This manifestation of God
is in the order of Person, *of the uncreated true self.* Our
creation as persons is our call to become perfectly like God's
likeness to himself. Our very existence as a created person
is a created subsisting relationship of love to Love, of
awareness to Awareness.

Contemplation can be validly seen as a human act carried on at a specific time by a specific individual. Likewise, contemplation certainly has deep implications in the daily life of the one who engages in it. But relative to all of that, contemplation of itself is not

> something infused by God into a created subject, so much as God living in God and identifying a created life with his own life so that there is nothing left of any significance but God living in God. . . . God alone is left. He is the "I" who acts there. He is the one Who loves and knows and rejoices.[12]

Who can attain such a union as this? It seems so esoteric, so beyond the average person, that it ought to be reserved for those living on cliff tops being fed daily by a raven. It seems, in fact, an impossible attainment. The point is well made, for it is indeed impossible when viewed from our own poverty and blindness. But "with God all things are possible."

Contemplation is God's gift and he gives his gifts to the poor and the lowly. Contemplatives are poor not simply because they realize that they are weak sinners totally dependent on God, but also because in contemplation itself there is no embellishment of the ego at all. Merton observes:

> the separate entity that is *you* apparently disappears and nothing seems to be left but a pure freedom indistinguishable from infinite Freedom, love identified with Love. Not two loves, one waiting for the other, striving for the other, seeking for the other, but Love Loving in freedom.[13]

A person drawn to contemplative prayer is drawn to the edge of an unseen abyss. He waits, held by a barrier that is not there, expecting everything out of nothing. There

is darkness and in the darkness a presence that stirs the
waters and creates a deeper emptiness. God empties out
the contents of the ego self until all is an empty expectancy.

And then when the gift finally is given,

> you do not take the step; you do not know the
> transition; you do not fall into anything. You do
> not go anywhere, and so you do not know the
> way by which you got there or the way by which
> you came back afterward. You are certainly not
> lost. You do not fly. There is no space, or there
> is all space: it makes no difference.[14]

"It makes no difference." It makes all the difference.
You are only who you are, yet you are "carried away by
the same wind that blows all these people down the street,
like pieces of paper and dead leaves in all directions."[15]
We are only who we are, yet who we are is God being God.
God loving and knowing himself in us not as vessels of his
knowledge and love but as his very love and knowledge,
his very self, created in us as persons.

The insight arises as an obscure yet deep realization
in faith that our ultimate identity is hidden in the secret of
God's identity. Though no longer contained in the confining perimeters of questions and answers, we find ourselves to be a kind of question, a question which only God
can answer:

> The Father is a Holy Spirit, but He is named
> Father. The Son is a Holy Spirit, but He is
> named Son. The Holy Spirit has a Name which
> is known only to the Father and the Son. But can
> it be that when He takes us to Himself, and
> unites us to the Father through the Son, He takes
> upon Himself, in us, our own secret name? Is it
> possible that we come to know, for ourselves, the
> name of the Holy Spirit when we receive from

Him the revelation of our own identity in Him?
I can ask these questions, but not answer them.[16]

The insight is the shattering realization that God is God, that he knows himself perfectly in us and that he calls us to know ourselves perfectly in Him. We are called as persons to know God with the "mind of Christ," that is, to know him by virtue of our existence as a relationship of perfect likeness to the Father.

The insight is a light in the darkness. It is a foreshadowing of our ultimate self that even now, though hidden and in becoming, is one with God. Thus we pray, though in the body or out of the body we cannot say, for "only God can say" (2 Cor 12:2). We pray in the new body of the Christ-self that has arisen from our old self, once buried in corruption (cf. 1 Cor 15). We pray in hope that one day who we are will be brought to full perfection. One day (a day that dawns from within the horizon of Christ's tomb) "we will be like him, for we shall see him as he is" (1 Jn 3:26).

We will never have this insight into the true self as long as we try to "have" an insight and then cling to what we think we have. Trying to have the insight is like trying to swallow the sky. The insight is that we are the insight. The insight is that there is nothing to acquire, for there is no one to acquire it. There is no insight other than the self we always have been, yet did not recognize. We suddenly realize that we had it all along.

We suddenly see the true self in an old woman pulling weeds, in a rose bush heavy with blossoms sagging in a summer storm. We hear the true self in a squeaky gate swinging in the wind. We hear it in our next breath. We touch it in our reaching out to our brother and sister. And we see, hear and touch the true self not by mystifying everything but by simply letting each thing be. Each thing is only

what it is, and in that alone each thing is a manifestation
of the ALL from whom all came, in whom all is sustained,
and to whom all returns.

The story of King Midas and his magic touch is an apt
image of the false mystic who wishes to gain something
not had by others, to see what others do not see. Midas
attained his coveted desire. He turned all he touched into
gold—even his daughter! And a golden daughter is no
daughter. A golden daughter is a dead daughter. It is gold
cast into the vestige of a hellish nightmare.

Contemplation is not an experience to be gained but
an eternal identity to be realized. It "only becomes an
experience in a man's memory."[17] As looked back upon
from within the context of the experiential self it bears
some resemblance to "something that happened." But this
appearance must not be claimed as a victory or everything
is lost, and Adam eats the forbidden fruit all over again.

Some hint of the nature of the contemplative insight
into the true self is seen in the following words of Merton,
which he wrote while alone in his hermitage in the middle
of the night,

> One might say I had decided to marry the
> silence of the forest. The sweet dark warmth of
> the whole world will have to be my wife. Out of
> the heart of that dark warmth comes the secret
> that is heard only in silence, but is the root of all
> the secrets that are whispered by all lovers in
> their beds all over the world. So perhaps I have
> an obligation to preserve the stillness, the silence,
> the poverty, the virginal point of pure nothingness
> which is at the center of all other loves. I attempt
> to cultivate this plant without comment in the
> middle of the night and water it with psalms and
> prophecies in silence. It becomes the most rare
> of all the trees in the garden, at once the pri-
> mordial paradise tree, the *axis mundi,* the cosmic

axle and the Cross. *Nulla silva talem profert.*
There is only one such tree. It cannot be multi-
plied. It is not interesting.[18]

This tree, this center, is not interesting. Interesting
things are on the circumference of the circle being developed by and threatened by other interesting things. Our
false self feeds upon and needs such things. It is itself interesting as it now gloats over this conquest and is crushed
by that defeat.

But the true self tires easily of such interesting things.
It does not deny them. It does not deny anything, nor affirm
anything, but stands at that point which is the center beyond
both affirmation and negation. The true self thirsts for its
own element. It thirsts for the water that springs up from
within us. It desires to sit beneath the paradise tree which
is No thing, which is not this or that, but the underlying
reality, the ultimate meaning of all that is.

Our silent prayer is poor, yet its poverty is its wealth
if we offer our poverty to God. Our silent prayer is empty,
yet its emptiness makes it full if we open ourselves to God
who, upon the cross, showed us that fullness is emptiness—
and upon the emptiness all things depend.

III

Nothing is solely what it appears to be. Appearances
are but appearances and the one who stops at appearances
is like a hungry man who eats only the skin of the apple.
A contemplative spirit is not content with a superficiality
that rests in what seems to be. Rather, illumined by faith,
cleansed by compunction and dread, the contemplative
journeys within, to discover that "if you descend into the
depths of your own spirit . . . and arrive somewhere near
the center of what you are, you are confronted with the

inescapable truth that, at the very roots of your existence, you are in constant and immediate and inescapable contact with the Infinite power of God."[19]

And how does God display his power? Above all, by existence itself. The roots of your existence find their nourishment by drawing upon God as "he who is existence." "He Who Is" sustains us in many ways, but above all he sustains us in existence. Our reality is truly our own, given to us by God, but it is nevertheless a received reality, it is the gift of our very existence drawing upon Existence.

As water pours forth from a vessel we pour forth from God in emptiness. He says "be" to us, and his word is the gift that makes us be. This has profound implications with regard to a central aspect of the life of prayer. It means that if we draw close to the roots of our own existence, to the naked being of ourself, we will find ourselves at that point where God and ourselves unite in ontological communion.

There is a small village through which flows a river from which all the inhabitants draw their sustenance. One day a child follows the river up through the thickly wooded hillside. After many hours, alone and exhausted, he follows the river into the shadows of a solitary glen. And there is the Source. There, from the hidden, virginal opening, silently surges forth the icy life-giving water from which he has drawn his life and refreshment all the days of his life. He lowers himself slowly and gently and drinks— knowing the river fully for the first time, for he communes with it at its source.

Once we enter into ourselves and discover an awareness of our own existence we discover a new vantage point from which we gaze out at the world as if for the first time. We discover that a tree simply *is*, prior to being tall or short, or even prior to being a tree. The tree *is*, for *He who is* communicates to it something of his own infinite actuality.

God communicates to the tree its being, that is, both its act of existence and its treeness, its unique identity as created by God.

This vision is not apprehended as a theory but as an irreversible and immediate intuition:

> Let us remind ourselves that another, metaphysical, consciousness is still available to modern man. It starts not from the thinking and self-aware subject but from Being, ontologically seen to be beyond and prior to the subject-object division. Underlying the subjective experience of the individual self there is an experience of Being. This is totally different from an experience of self-consciousness. It is completely non-objective. It has in it none of the split and alienation that occurs when the subject becomes aware of itself as a quasi-object. The consciousness of Being . . . is an immediate experience that goes beyond reflexive awareness. It is not "consciousness of" but *pure consciousness,* in which the subject as such "disappears."[20]

In the immediate intuitive awareness of existence, a tree and I are seen as one, for that act by which the tree is and that by which I am is one and the same act; namely, the act of existence. Surely, the tree's act of existence is proper to the tree; it is the tree that exists. Likewise, my act of existence is unique to me. But existence itself is the one common denominator that binds all together in the unity of being.

Thus, in this mode of vision, there is no subject-object division, for the vision enters into the flow of being which is "beyond and prior to subject-object division." It enters into the flow of existence as He-Who-Is-Existence gives existence to all that exists. Thus this mode of vision is the vision of the true self which subsists in God as presence created in Presence, as love created in Love.

We must not reserve this awareness to the halls of academia, where philosophers ponder metaphysical questions with a density and complexity beyond the grasp of most. In fact, no academic, scientific exercise in and of itself, can yield the insight referred to by Merton. It is true that academic study can make the insight more precise. It provides a vocabulary with which to discuss it with others, but

> One who apprehends being as such apprehends it as an act which is utterly beyond a complete scientific explanation. To apprehend being is an act of contemplation and philosophical wisdom rather than the fruit of scientific analysis. It is in fact a gift given to few. Anyone can say: "This is a tree; that is a man." But how few are ever struck by the realization of the real import of what is really meant by is?

> Sometimes it is given to children and to simple people (and the "intellectual" may indeed be an essentially simple person, contrary to all the myths about him—for only the stupid are disqualified from true simplicity) to experience a direct intuition of being. Such an intuition is simply an immediate grasp of one's own inexplicable personal reality in one's own incommunicable act of existing![21]

In the moment of this existential realization of being the statement "I Am" takes on an explosive, shattering, yet peace-giving force. In utter simplicity, we intuitively realize within ourselves that our existence, though truly our own, is to He Who Is as the waves are to the sea, as the light is to the flame. Our prayer becomes our basking in this light, our being quietly warmed by it, our being consumed by it. Our prayer becomes our silent sinking in the sea of being that is at once God and ourselves. Contemplation is that mode of awareness in which we realize:

> His presence is present in my own presence.
> If I am, then He is. And in knowing that I am, if
> I penetrate to the depths of my own existence and
> my own present reality, the indefinable "am" that
> is myself in its deepest roots, then through this
> deep center I pass into the infinite "I Am" which
> is the very Name of the Almighty.

> My knowledge of myself in silence (not by
> reflection on my self, but by penetration to the
> mystery of my true self which is beyond words
> and concepts because it is utterly particular)
> opens out into the silence and the "subjectivity"
> of God's own self.

> The grace of Christ identifies me with the
> "engraved word" (*insitum verbum*) which is
> Christ living in me. *Vivit in me Christus.* Identi-
> fication by love leads to knowledge, recognition,
> intimate and obscure but vested with an inexpres-
> sible certainty known only in contemplation.[22]

In ways known only to God, the one seeking God in silence unexpectedly falls through the barriers of division and duplicity to discover that

> where contemplation becomes what it is really
> meant to be, it is no longer something infused by
> God into a created subject, so much as God liv-
> ing in God and identifying a created life with His
> own Life so that there is nothing left of any sig-
> nificance but God living in God.[23]

This "disappearance" is the antithesis of any form of loss of self. Rather it is an expression of the true self's final consummation as a created capacity for perfect union with God. Thus, this disappearance is actually a manifestation of ourselves as radically one with God. The only self that actually vanishes is our false self, the self we thought ourselves to be, the self conceived in Adam's acceptance of the serpent's odious lie. Within the context of this contemplative awareness, we actualize in the roots of our own consciousness the truth of Jesus' words: "He who loses his life shall find it."

Our false self is extinguished in this realization. And our external self, our social, psychological, emotional self is given a new freedom, for we are able to place our observable self in its proper relationship to God:

> The empirical self is seen by comparison to be "nothing," that is to say contingent, evanescent, relatively unreal, real only in relation to its source and end in God, considered not as object but as free ontological source of one's own existence and subjectivity.[24]

The contemplative realizes that the ego-self is

> not final or absolute; it is a provisional self-construction which exists, for practical purposes, only in a sphere of relativity. Its existence has meaning in so far as it does not become fixated or centered upon itself as ultimate, learns to function not as its own center but 'from God' and 'for others.'[25]

These reflections on being and our apparent "disappearance" in the wake of contemplative prayer open the way for us to recall once again the themes of death, dread, emptiness and the "dark night" which so frequently occur in Merton's writings. Approaching these themes at the level of being and from the standpoint of contemplative insight into the true self can help us reach a yet deeper grasp of Merton's notions of the true self and the nature of contemplative union.

IV

Death is the Gordian knot of human existence. Once we accept the fact that our ego-self is not final or absolute, we open the door to a full, existential acknowledgement of our own impending death. Merton writes,

> putting it in the form of a question, it comes out like "Who are you when you do not exist?"

> Is this question an absurd one? On the contrary, it is I think a most attractive and fascinating one because of the obscure promises that it contains and because the answer to it can never be grasped by the mind. It is a question into which one must plunge himself entirely before it can make any sense—and that means, in a way, plunging entirely into nothingness, not just struggling with the *idea* of nothingness.

> When the question presents itself as an alien chill, it is saying something important: it is an accusation. It is telling me that I am too concerned with trivialities. That life is losing itself in trifles which cannot bear inspection in the face of death. That I am evading my chief responsibility. That I must begin to face the deepest of all decisions—the "answer of death"—the acceptance of the death sentence—and with joy, because of the victory of Christ.[26]

As we have seen repeatedly in the pages of this book, the themes of death, emptiness, dread and loss form one of the leitmotifs in Merton's spirituality. This has nothing to do with a macabre fascination with the grave, but rather represents a ruthless campaign against giving way to all "trifles which cannot bear inspection in the face of death." This does not mean becoming a spiritual superman who rises above the banal trivialities of the masses. The contemplative's life contains all the countless little concerns that are part and parcel of daily human existence. But Merton's frequent recalling of death has much to do with not breaking faith with God's call that arises from the obscure depths of silent prayer. His concern with death has much to do with recognizing each thing for what it is and acknowledging that no object, no experience, no achievement can sustain me in existence, and, therefore, to be authentic I must struggle to be true to "my chief responsibility" of searching for a life that "bears inspection in the face of death."

But there is more to Merton's concern with death than his existentialist's quest for authenticity. Merton's concern with death results from his concern for love. Any lover, anyone who has tasted something of the riches of friendship, knows by experience the paradox that communion with the beloved necessitates a letting go, a surrender, a *death* to the self-contained, autonomous ego-self. A kind of nakedness is called for, a risk that accompanies our letting another into the inner recesses of our heart and our own simultaneous ecstasy, our going out of ourselves into the other, thus making a "you and I" into an "us." Thus, two become one only in a mutual death that unfolds and makes possible a simultaneous mutual consummation of an unknown "self" born of love.

This phenomenological approach toward the intrinsic relationship between communion and death to self can be analogously applied to the experience of contemplative union with God. Douglas Steere in his introduction to

Merton's book, *Contemplative Prayer,* makes an astute remark on this point. He writes:

> The deepest prayer at its nub is a perpetual sur-
> render to God . . . all meditation and specific
> acts of prayer might be seen as preparations and
> purifications to ready us for this never ending
> yielding. Yet what is so often concealed is that
> there is a terrible dread that sweeps over me in
> the face of such an expectation. If I am what I
> think myself to be and God is as I have pictured
> him to be, then perhaps I could bear to risk it.
> But what if he should turn out to be other than I
> have pictured him, and what if, in his piercing
> presence, whole layers of what I have known
> myself to be should dissolve away and an utterly
> unpredictable encounter should take place?[27]

In prayer our whole being waits to be "taken by God and seen no more." In prayer, like the stars before the rising sun, all the burdens of our autonomous self disperse before the "piercing presence" of God. God unclothes, undoes us, "prunes away every branch that does not bear fruit." He even takes God away from us (that is, all our assumptions, convictions, our ideas of what he is like). He even takes away our self from us (that is, all we have thought ourselves to be). He draws us into a sphere of emptiness in which there appears to be no one left, neither God nor a self to know him. As Merton puts it,

> Contemplation is the highest and most para-
> doxical form of self-realization, attained by ap-
> parent self-annihilation.[28]

Elsewhere, Merton assures us that

> The reason for this (loss of self) is not that
> the person loses his metaphysical or even physical

status, or regresses into non-entity, but rather
that his *real* status is quite other than what em-
pirically appears to be his status.[29]

This disappearance, this annihilation is all a matter
of appearances as seen through the eyes of the false self.
The annihilation is only apparent, for the self being annihilated is itself only apparent. It is a self without God, that
is, a self that can never exist. What is annihilated is our
false self, our external self made absolute, the imposter,
the mask (persona), the liar we think we are but are not.
The annihilation therefore is not annihilation at all, for
nothing real or genuine is annihilated. Rather, what is
genuine is affirmed as our psychological, historical, social
self and placed in its true relationship to God. All that is
annihilated is the illusion of the self that cannot bear God's
presence, save as an idol fabricated for the ego's own glori-
fication. It is this "self" that is "annihilated" through God's
merciful love.

The annihilation is merciful for it, in fact, is the antithesis of annihilation. It is rather an obscure, inexplicable
foretaste in faith of our final consummation as created
persons. It is the mystery of the cross creatively at work
in the foundations of consciousness, recreating our awareness that we might know God as he knows himself.

This is why Christ came that through him and in the
Spirit we might find our fulfillment in union with the Father.
Merton relates this contemplative transformation of con-
sciousness to the whole of Christian life, saying:

> This dynamic of emptying and of transcen-
> dence accurately defines the transformation of the
> Christian consciousness in Christ. It is a kenotic
> transformation, an emptying of all the contents
> of the ego-consciousness to become a void in
> which the light of God or the glory of God, the

full radiation of the infinite reality of His Being and Love are manifested.[30]

The person we are is not limited to the individual we are. The identity of the individual is determined by a host of historical, cultural, psychological and genetic factors. The person, while embracing and being one with all this, is not determined by anything, but rather transcends everything in its radical union of likeness to God.

Contemplation is that act in which what we do is who we are. Contemplation is our person, our true self truly (albeit obscurely) actualizing itself as a self made to become perfectly like God. This actualization affirms in us all that is genuine in relation to our historical, everyday self-awareness. This self-actualization of ourselves as one with God is experienced as a mystical death which brings us to realize that:

> when we lose our special, separate cultural and religious identity—the "self" or "persona" that is the subject of virtues as well as visions, that perfects itself by good works, that advances in the practice of piety—(it is then) that Christ is finally born in us in the highest sense.[31]

This loss, this going out, this ecstasy is not a going out from one form of self-containment into another, as though we were but pouring the precious fluid of our being into a bigger and more richly embellished container marked "mysticism." No. Rather the going out is a going out into Being itself. The awareness of our *being* is made one with the *Being* of God. It is in contemplation that God becomes ALL in ALL in us as created persons called to perfect union with God.

"The transformation of the Christian consciousness in Christ," the "emptying of all the contents of ego-consciousness" is thus not a matter of psychology but of ontology. The contemplative's "experience" of self-emptying is a manifestation, a revelation of the "emptiness" of God. Merton writes:

> The ALL is nothing, for if it were to be a single thing separated from all other things, it would not be ALL. This precisely is the liberty I have always sought: the freedom of being subject to nothing and therefore to live in ALL, through ALL, for ALL, by Him who is ALL. In Christian terms, this is to live "in Christ" and by the "Spirit of Christ," for the Spirit is like the wind, blowing where He pleases, and He is the Spirit of Truth. The "Truth shall make you free."

> But if the truth is to make me free, I must also let go my hold upon myself, and not retain the semblance of a self which is an object of a "thing." I, too, must be no-thing. And when I am no-thing I am in the ALL, and Christ lives in me.[32]

If God were something (some thing) he would not be ALL, for we would have but to find one grain of sand to find some thing he is not and thereby deprive him of being ALL. But since God is nothing (no thing) he moves in perfect freedom as the ground, the source, the fulfillment, the no-thing that sustains all things. We are "real" because we are in existence. God, however, is not in existence, but is rather Existence itself. He *is* that by which we are.

In God's no-thing-ness is his perfect freedom. He is not this; he is not that. He is ALL in all. Merton tells us, in effect, that the call to contemplative prayer is a call from God to realize that, as created persons made in God's image, we too are no-thing. As persons we shall find our fulfillment not in any thing but only in a total union and identification with God in love.

The emptiness, the dread and the darkness of prayer are echoes of this call from God. Our helplessness, our sinfulness, and our pettiness are invitations, graces, and calls, not to despair but to a total abandonment and emptying of ourselves into the infinite power and presence of God which are manifested to us through our share in Christ's cross.

How strange God's ways are! He calls us to a union we do not understand. He calls us to a place of encounter which we cannot find. We search and search. Our silence reveals to us not a garden of delights but an awful nothingness. God leaves us in an awful emptiness. All our initial enthusiastic notions of prayer deteriorate into an acknowledgement of our utter superficiality and lack of authenticity before God. We can only throw ourselves completely on his mercy. We can only wait in the darkness and cry out for our salvation. We can but trust that God's love is such that our sinfulness does not even matter. We can only have faith. We can only believe that in Christ God has already spied us afar off returning repentant to his home. In Christ God has already rushed out to meet us, fallen upon us and kissed us. We can only accept that our poverty is so utterly deep that God himself will have to be our inheritance. Our darkness is so intense God himself will have to be our light.

And it is to this that God leads us. It is here in this no-where that we are brought to no-thing. It is here that God reveals to us that he truly is God and that we are created to become who we are by becoming perfectly like him. It is here that poverty reaches its supreme moment, for it is here that there is no longer anyone left to own any thing. Here there is only Presence, only gracious emptiness, a Freedom and Love that forms a "circle whose circumference is nowhere and whose center is everywhere."[33] The contemplative is drawn into this circle by a divine com-

passion. The contemplative is brought to this fontal No-
where to be given All by being dispossessed of all that is
partial and passing. Here we understand with a new clarity
what everyone at least vaguely and unconsciously suspects:

> There is only one problem on which all my exis-
> tence, my peace, my happiness depend: to dis-
> cover myself in discovering God. If I find Him
> I will find myself and if I find my true self I will
> find Him.[34]

Words fail to describe this unveiling of the emptiness
of uncreated Being which forms the root of our identity as
persons made in God's image:

> Desert and void. The uncreated is waste
> and emptiness to the creature. Not even sand.
> Not even stone. Not even darkness and night.
> A burning wilderness would at least be "some-
> thing." It burns and is wild. But the Uncreated
> is no something. Waste. Emptiness. Total pov-
> erty of the Creator: yet from this poverty springs
> *everything*. The waste is inexhaustible. Infinite
> Zero. Everything wants to return to it and can-
> not. For who can return "nowhere"? But for
> each of us there is a point of nowhereness in the
> middle of movement, a point of nothingness in
> the midst of being: the incomparable point, not
> to be discovered by insight. If you seek it you do
> not find it. If you stop seeking, it is there. But
> you must not turn to it. Once you become aware
> of yourself as seeker, you are lost. But if you
> are content to be lost you will be found without
> knowing it, precisely because you are lost, for you
> are, at last, nowhere.[35]

A life of contemplative prayer is above all a life. But
it is a life that is truly a life lived in such a way that we

come to realize that, "whatever you do, every act however small, can teach you everything. Provided you see who it is that is acting."[36]

And seeing who is acting becomes possible with the recognition that,

> At the center of our being is a point of nothingness which is untouched by sin and by illusion, a point of pure truth, a point or spark which belongs entirely to God, which is never at our disposal, from which God disposes of our lives, which is inaccessible to the fantasies of our own mind or the brutalities of our own will. This little point of nothingness and of *absolute poverty* is the pure glory of God in us. It is so to speak His name written in us, as our poverty, as our indigence, as our dependence, as our sonship. It is like a pure diamond, blazing with the invisible light of heaven. It is in everybody, and if we could see it we would see these billions of points of light coming together in the face and blaze of a sun that would make all the darkness and cruelty of life vanish completely. . . I have no program for this seeing. It is only given. But the gate of heaven is everywhere.[37]

The following lengthy quote, written by Merton just before his death, echoes with the insight into the true self. The quote serves as a fitting conclusion of this small book and the message it has tried to convey:

> The Three doors (they are one door).
>
> 1) The door of emptiness. Of no-where. Of no place for a self, which cannot be entered by a self. And therefore is of no use to someone who is going somewhere. Is it a door at all? The door of no-door.

2) The door without sign, without indicator, without information. Not particularized. Hence no one can say of it "This is *it*. This is *the door*." It is not recognizable as a door. It is not led up to by other things pointing to it: "We are not it, but that is it—the door." No signs saying "Exit." No use looking for indications. Any door with a sign saying "Not-door." Or even "No Exit."

3) The door without wish. The undesired. The unplanned door. The door never expected. Never wanted. Not desirable as a door. Not a joke, not a trap door. Not select. Not exclusive. Not for a few. Not for many. Not *for*. Door without aim. Door without end. Does not respond to a key—so do not imagine you have a key. Do not have your hopes on possession of the key.

There is no use asking for it. Yet you must ask. Who? For what? When you have asked for a list of all the doors, this one is not on the list. When you have asked the numbers of all the doors, this one is without a number. Do not be deceived into thinking this door is merely hard to find and difficult to open. When sought it fades. Recedes. Diminishes. Is nothing. There is no threshold. No footing. It is not empty space. It is neither this world nor another. It is not based on anything. Because it has no foundation, it is the end of sorrow. Nothing remains to be done. Therefore there is no threshold, no step, no advance, no recession, no entry, no nonentry. Such is the door that ends all doors; the unbuilt, the impossible, the undestroyed, through which all the fires go when they have "gone out."

Christ said, "I am the door." The nailed door. The cross, they nail the door shut with death. The resurrection: "You see, I am *not* a door." "Why do you look up to heaven?" *Attolite portas principes vestras* (Lift up your heads, O gates. Psalm 23:9). For what? The King of Glory. *Ego sum ostium* (I am the door. Jn 10:7). I am the opening, the "shewing," the revelation, the door of light, the Light itself. "I am the Light," and the light is in the world from the beginning. (It seemed to be darkness.) [38]

This one door is the door of the Palace of Nowhere. It is the door of God. It is our very self, our true self called by God to perfect union with himself. And it is through this door we secretly enter in responding to the saving call to:

"Come with me to the Palace of Nowhere where all the many things are one."

Notes

INTRODUCTION

1. Thomas Merton, *The Sign of Jonas* (New York: Harcourt, Brace and Co., 1953). Edition cited: Image Books, Doubleday and Company, 1956, p. 26.

2. Thomas Merton, *New Seeds of Contemplation* (New York: New Directions, 1961). Edition cited: New Directions Paperbook, 1972, p. 5. Hereafter indicated as NSC.

3. Thomas Merton, *Spiritual Direction and Meditation* (Collegeville, Minnesota: Liturgical Press, 1960). p. 21.

4. NSC, p. 36.

5. Merton, *A Thomas Merton Reader,* ed. Thomas P. McDonnell (New York: Harcourt, Brace and World, Inc. 1961). Edition cited: Image Books, Doubleday and Company, 1974. p. 213.

6. NSC, p. 12.

7. Ibid., p. 4.

8. Both *Raids on the Unspeakable* and *Bread in the Wilderness* are titles of books written by Merton.

9. Merton, *Mystics and Zen Masters* (New York: Farrar, Straus and Giroux, 1967). p. 42.

10. Merton, *Zen and the Birds of Appetite* (New York: New Directions, 1968). pp. 13-14. Hereafter indicated as ZBA.

11. Merton, "The Inner Experience: Notes on Contemplation" (unpublished). p. 6.

CHAPTER I:

THE FOUNDATION OF THE FALSE SELF

1. Thomas Merton, *The Way of Chuang Tzu* (New York: New Directions, 1965). p. 77.
2. NSC, pp. 33-34.
3. Ibid., pp. 35-36.
4. Merton, *Contemplative Prayer* (New York: Herder and Herder, 1969). Edition cited: Image Books, Doubleday and Company, 1971, p. 70. Hereafter indicated as CP.
5. NSC, p. 34.
6. Merton, *The New Man* (New York: Farrar, Straus and Cudahy, 1961). pp. 117-118. Hereafter indicated as NM.
7. NSC, pp. 34-35.
8. Ibid., p. 35.
9. NM, p. 111.
10. Ibid., pp. 118-119.

CHAPTER II:

THE TRUE SELF IN THE WORLD

1. CP, pp. 38-39.
2. Thomas Merton, "Conscience of a Christian Monk," *Life and Contemplation*, Tape 4A, The Thomas Merton Tapes, ed. Norm Kramer (Chappaqua, New York: Electronic Paperbacks, 1972).
3. Thomas Merton, *Contemplation in a World of Action* (New York: Doubleday and Company, 1971). p. 7.
4. *A Thomas Merton Reader,* pp. 458-459.
5. *Contemplation in a World of Action,* pp. 154-155.
6. Merton, *Conjectures of a Guilty Bystander* (New York: Doubleday and Company, 1966). p. 71. Hereafter indicated as CGB.
7. Thomas Merton, *Disputed Questions* (New York: Farrar, Straus and Cudahy, 1960). Edition cited: Menter-Omega, 1965. pp. 146-147.
8. CGB, pp. 241-242.
9. Ibid., p. 36.

10. Merton, "Thomas Merton's View of Monasticism," in *The Asian Journal,* ed. Naomi Burton, Brother Patrick Hart and James Laughlin (New York: New Directions, 1973). pp. 305-306.

11. Ibid., p. 307.

12. *Contemplation in a World of Action,* p. 143.

13. Merton, "Learning to Live," in *University on the Heights,* ed. W. First (New York: Doubleday and Company, 1969). Text used: for private circulation only, p. 7.

14. Thomas Merton, "Obstacles to Union with God," *Life and God's Love,* Tape 6B, The Thomas Merton Tapes, ed. Norm Kramer (Chappaqua, New York: Electronic Paperbacks, 1972).

15. Loc. cit.

16. *Contemplation in a World of Action,* pp. 155-156.

CHAPTER III:

THE TRUE SELF IN RELIGIOUS SEARCHING

1. "Concerning the Collection in the Bellarmine College Library— A statement, November 10, 1963." Merton Studies Center, I (1971). p. 3.

2. Johannes Baptist Metz, *Poverty of Spirit* (New York: Newman Press, 1968). p. 28.

3. Thomas Merton, "As Man to Man," *Cistercian Studies, IV* (1969), pp. 93-94.

4. Merton, *Redeeming the Time* (London: Burns and Oates, 1966). p. 40.

5. NSC, p. 64.

6. "Obstacles to Union With God," tape.

7. CBG, p. 157.

8. Ibid., p. 30.

9. "Day of a Stranger," in *A Thomas Merton Reader.* Text cited: For private circulation only, p. 4.

10. "Obstacles to Union With God," tape.

11. CGB, p. 157.

12. Thomas Merton, *Thoughts in Solitude* (New York: Farrar, Straus and Cudahy, 1956). pp. 52-53.

13. "Obstacles to Union With God," tape.

14. Ibid.

15. Ibid.
16. NM, p. 29.
17. Ibid., pp. 23-24.
18. Ibid., p. 35.
19. Loc. cit.
20. Ibid., p. 24.
21. CGB, p. 131.
22. *Thoughts in Solitude,* p. 97.
23. CP, p. 89.
24. NM, p. 37.
25. ZBA, p. 76.
26. Ibid., pp. 76-77.
27. Ibid., p. 77.
28. *Mystics and Zen Masters,* p. 22.
29. Loc. cit.
30. Ibid., p. 23.
31. Loc. cit.
32. ZBA, p. 73.
33. Ibid., p. 77.
34. Ibid., p. 75.

CHAPTER IV:

THE REALIZATION OF THE TRUE SELF

1. Merton, "The Inner Experience: Notes on Contemplation," p. 16.
2. Loc. cit.
3. ZBA, p. IX.
4. "The Inner Experience: Notes on Contemplation," pp. 4-5.
5. CP, p. 94.
6. "The Inner Experience: Notes on Contemplation," p. 5.
7. CP, p. 34.
8. Thomas Merton, *The Living Bread* (New York: Farrar, Straus and Cudahy, 1956). p. 4.
9. Merton, "Conference on Prayer," *Sisters Today,* XLI (1970). Text used for private circulation only, p. 2.

10. ZBA, A statement made by Eckhart, quoted by D. T. Suzuki and here referred to by Merton. p. 57.

11. NSC, pp. 134-135.

12. "Conference on Prayer," p. 5.

13. *A Thomas Merton Reader*, p. 515.

14. "As Man to Man," p. 94.

15. *A Thomas Merton Reader*, p. 314.

16. *The Living Bread,* p. 68.

17. CP, p. 30.

18. Ibid., p. 94.

19. Thomas Merton, *The Seven Storey Mountain* (New York: Harcourt, Brace and Company, 1948). Edition cited: Signet Books, New American Library, Inc. p. 409.

20. "The Inner Experience: Notes on Contemplation," p. 39.

21. Loc. cit.

22. CP, p. 68.

23. NSC, p. 60.

24. CP, p. 97.

25. Ibid., pp. 109-110.

26. Ibid., pp. 43-44.

27. "The Inner Experience: Notes on Contemplation," pp. 105-106.

28. Ibid., p. 104.

29. Ibid., p. 88.

30. Merton comments on this text using the Vulgate translation. The Vulgate is retained here in order to parallel Merton's commentary.

31. "The Inner Experience: Notes on Contemplation," p. 88.

32. "Day of a Stranger," in *A Thomas Merton Reader,* p. 436.

33. Ibid., p. 433.

34. Ibid., from portion found in edition for private circulation only, p. 7.

35. CP, p. 30. Here Merton is quoting Isaac of Niniveh.

36. "As Man to Man," p. 94.

37. Thomas Merton, *Bread in the Wilderness* (New York: New Directions, 1953). p. 76.

38. This term was used by Father Daniel Walsh, who played a significant role in Merton's conversion to the Church, his entrance into Gethsemani and his developing notion of the true self. For Father Walsh the term *transubjectivity* is applicable not only to the three divine persons of the Trinity (subsisting in a perfect transubjective unity in the Divine Essence) but also to our own identities as created persons grounded in a transubjective unity with God. This transubjective unity is what Merton refers to as the true self.

39. David Steindl-Rast, "Man of Prayer," in *Thomas Merton, Monk: Monastic Tribute*. ed. Brother Patrick Hart (New York: Sheed and Ward, Inc., 1974). p. 80.

40. NSC, p. 281.

41. Thomas Merton, *What Are These Wounds? The Life of a Cistercian Mystic, Saint Lutgarde of Aywi'eres* (Milwaukee: Bruce, 1950). p. 14. This identical point is made by Saint John of the Cross in *The Ascent of Mount Carmel* 2, 5, 7, where he states: "When God grants this supernatural favor to the soul, so great a union is caused that all the things of both God and the soul become one in participant transformation, and the soul appears to be God more than a soul. Indeed, it is God by participation. Yet truly, its being (even though transformed) is naturally as distinct from God's as it was before. . ."

42. "Day of a Stranger" in *A Thomas Merton Reader,* p. 433.

43. CGB, p. 131.

44. David Steindl-Rast, "Man of Prayer," pp. 83-84.

45. Ibid., p. 82.

46. Merton, *Disputed Questions* (New York: Farrar, Straus and Cudahy, 1960). p. 160.

CHAPTER V:

THE INSIGHT

1. "Monastic Experience and East-West Dialogue," in *The Asian Journal*, pp. 315-316.

2. "Symbolism: Communication or Communion," in *Monastic Exchange,* Summer, 1970. p. 6.

3. Loc. cit.

4. "Monastic Experience and East-West Dialogue," p. 4.

5. *Mystics and Zen Masters*, p. 20.

6. ZBA, p. 53.

7. CGB, p. 131.

8. *Sign of Jonas*, p. 351.

9. *Mystics and Zen Masters*, p. 33.

10. NSC, p. 279.

11. Loc. cit.

12. Ibid., pp. 284-287.

13. Ibid., p. 283.

14. Loc. cit.

15. Edward Rice, *The Man in the Sycamore Tree: The Good Times and Hard Life of Thomas Merton* (New York: Doubleday and Company, Inc., 1970). p. 141.

16. "The Inner Experience: Notes on Contemplation," p. 35.

17. NSC, p. 283.

18. "Day of a Stranger" in *A Thomas Merton Reader*, pp. 434-435.

19. "The Contemplative Life: Its Meaning and Necessity," *Dublin Review*, CCXXII (1949), p. 28.

20. ZBA, pp. 23-24.

21. CGB, pp. 200-201.

22. *Thoughts in Solitude*, p. 70.

23. NSC, p. 284.

24. ZBA, p. 26.

25. Ibid., p. 24.

26. CGB, pp. 239-240.

27. CP, p. 13.

28. NM, p. 19.

29. ZBA, p. 76.

30. Ibid., p. 75.

31. Ibid., p. 12.

32. "Introducing a Book," *Queens Work*, LVI (1964), p. 10.

33. ZBA, p. 65.

34. NSC, p. 36.

35. Thomas Merton, *Cables to the Ace or Familiar Liturgies of Misunderstanding* (New York: New Directions, 1967). p. 58.

36. "Learning to Live," p. 10.

37. CGB, p. 142.

38. *The Asian Journal*, pp. 153-155.